LIVERPOOL

A LANDSCAPE HISTORY

LIVERPOOL

A LANDSCAPE HISTORY

MARTIN GREANEY

To Mum and Dad, and my brother Stephen, who have encouraged me every step of the way. To my wife, Sue, for her love and support in everything at which I try my hand. And to the memory of Mr Dewsnap, the best history teacher, bar none.

First published 2013
Reprinted 2014

The History Press
The Mill, Brimscombe Port
Stroud, Gloucestershire, GL5 2QG
www.thehistorypress.co.uk

British Library Cataloguing in Publication Data.
A catalogue record for this book is available from the British Library.

ISBN 978 0 7524 8833 2

Typesetting and origination by The History Press
Printed in Great Britain

CONTENTS

PROLOGUE

WHAT IS THE LANDSCAPE?

This book is all about Liverpool's 'historic landscape'. But it does more than simply discuss the history of the ground on which the city was built. The natural landscape shaped the history of Merseyside long before Liverpool was founded in 1207. The rivers, bogs, hills and valleys dictated where people could settle, and so affected the emerging politics from prehistory into the medieval period. Many of King John's reasons for establishing a new town on the north-west coast were related to the landscape's suitability for a sheltered harbour and a castle, as well as proximity to Ireland.

But even in the more modern age, when we think we are in command of nature, the development of the city depends on what has gone before. Old buildings need to come down before new ones can be built in their place. New motorways must cut through existing landscapes. Decisions on planning not only depend on where something needs to *go*, but also what is there right now. And decisions made about construction now will in turn affect future developments. We are perhaps only now coming to realise that our actions have repercussions for our descendents.

Therefore, this book is not just about the unwinding story of Liverpool and Merseyside, but also about the constant process of reinvention which the city has undergone and must continue to go through to develop and adapt to new circumstances. It tries to reveal why buildings were put where they still stand today, why roads simply peter out on the outskirts or why some shops seem half-buried in the pavement (read about the semi-basements in Chapter 5).

If this book succeeds in its aims, you will see Liverpool in a new light, or at least look at it with an eye for more detail than you did before. When you are next out in the city, look up above the shop fronts to understand the history of the road you are in. When an old wall remains in a new housing estate, follow it to see if its line gives clues as to its original use. Old maps are a great source for this kind of investigation and many are used throughout this volume. The photos I've taken for other illustrations go to show how much of this 'fossilised' history remains for the observant passer-by.

Even though there are dozens of interesting books out there covering Liverpool's history, this one differs in that it deals with the history of Liverpool itself, and the city more than the events which played out within it. Of course, it is difficult to write about the buildings, institutions and architectural innovations without mentioning the women and men who were involved, but they take a back seat to descriptions of why Liverpool looks the way it does, why it exists at all, and what was here before it. Because of this, the book can cover much older periods of time; periods for which our only way of investigating is to pull together the scattered clues from archaeological excavation, map analysis, and a little bit of geography, to show what it was like to live in the Merseyside landscape before Liverpool even existed.

The earliest chapters begin in a time when the land itself was being formed, when the bedrock was laid down before being sculpted by Ice Age glaciers. The story continues with the arrival of the first human communities, who left only scant traces in the landscape. These people seemed to look more intently towards their Irish and Atlantic European neighbours – to the sea – more than they did inland.

Later these isles were inhabited by British, Roman, Norse, German and Norman peoples, who added their own layers of history to the landscape, to mingle with those that came before. The landscape of south Lancashire (as it would become) was crucial to the way the medieval manors and farms developed. This is true on both a local and a national scale, and would continue to be so up to and beyond the time King John decided to create a borough here in 1207. When Liverpool was created, the location, the geography and the political situation of the area was crucial to John's choice to place his new town on the banks of the Mersey. Although this was a 'new' town, the landscape was by no means empty: there were farms, manor houses, a castle and power base in West Derby.

This is still an age when most of what we know of Liverpool comes from silent witnesses: archaeological objects and investigations. But, from the time when Liverpool grew in stature from a tiny fishing village into a bustling Tudor town in the sixteenth century, many more resources are available to tell us about this burgeoning urban area. This book will take you through the centuries when Liverpool first came into its own as a port, and became embroiled in the Civil War as a strategic objective. By this time Liverpool was starting to see itself on a par with the other great provincial towns of England: Bath, Ipswich, Bristol and Chester. Its ambitions grew and its landscape reflects these developments, with buildings, roads and fashionable squares aping those of London, Edinburgh and elsewhere. By 1800 Liverpool was a smart town attracting entrepreneurial businessmen, but on the horizon were the revolutionary changes which were sweeping Britain and the world.

Having developed into a port, and staked its future on pioneering wet dock technology, Liverpool suddenly found itself, during the Industrial Revolution, on the doorstep of the great manufacturing districts of northern England, on the main trade route to Europe and the Americas. Once again, geography – landscape – was on Liverpool's side, and it took advantage. By 1900 Liverpool was at the height of its powers – the biggest port outside London – and faced proudly across the Atlantic at her American cousins to whom she shipped countless souls from Ireland and elsewhere, and untold tonnes of cargo.

However, just as the landscape had been Liverpool's greatest ally in its rise to prominence, so landscape was its gravest enemy in the twentieth century. As a port it became a prime target for the German air force. After the Second World War manufacturing left Lancashire and Yorkshire; Europe, rather than America, was Britain's big trading partner. Liverpool was a specialist transport hub but had nothing to transport, and found it hard to adapt. The twentieth century was Liverpool's darkest but, towards the end, history came to save the city.

In the last twenty years of the twentieth century, and into the twenty-first, Liverpool's long and illustrious history and architecture, as well as the music, comedy and drama which emerged from its more infamous corners, came to dominate conversations about the town. It has become the 'birthplace' of the Beatles, and the 'home' of football. The accent borne of its many immigrants, its age-old global connections via the sea, and its famous sons and daughters from a hundred suburban backgrounds, sold Liverpool to a willing public, who came to love the city again.

So Liverpool was built on landscape foundations, grew strong on its geography and was populated by a people shaped by location. This book maps those changes over time, and reveals where the clues still remain for you to see them. If you live in the city, you may come to see Liverpool's history anew, but if you're just a visitor – or even if you've never been there – you may look at your own hometown in a new way; at how at every stage the landscape has been as much a historical force as the prime ministers, kings, queens, and ordinary people who have walked through it.

CHAPTER 1

FROM THE EARLIEST PREHISTORY TO THE FOUNDING OF LIVERPOOL

GEOLOGY AND THE LAST ICE AGE

Liverpool's historic landscape is built upon the geology which underlies it. To understand the history of Liverpool is firstly to understand the rock it was built upon, and from. The very oldest rocks beneath the city are Carboniferous (360 to 300 million years old) which consist of limestone and sandstone, and contain coal. These were formed from the decayed plant material laid down in wide, swampy river deltas, as this area formed part of the coastline at the time.

On top of this sit Triassic rocks (250 to 200 million years old) which were formed at the edge of an arid, desert mountain range. The softer Triassic rocks (such as the characteristic red sandstone of which much of Liverpool's older buildings are constructed) have been weathered into the Cheshire and Lancashire plains which sit to the north and south of Liverpool, while the harder Carboniferous rocks juts out to either side of the Triassic to form the Welsh uplands in the west and the foothills of the Pennines in the east.

As we're interested in the geology which influenced later history, it's worth pointing out that the geology provided many of the raw materials which went into building Liverpool or (via export) its wealth. Sand, clay, building stone, salt and underground water were all exploitable materials present in the ground across the region before Liverpool was founded. Coal could be found in great quantities in Wales and Lancashire to the east and west of Liverpool, but another, smaller, pocket was exposed in the grounds of Croxteth Hall.

These layers of rock form the foundations of the landscape, but relatively recently (in geological terms) this foundation was carved into new shapes. Around 12,000 years ago the whole of northern Europe was covered in ice up to 3 or 4km thick. It took the form of an expanded polar ice-cap which stretched, at its maximum, as far south in Britain as the Bristol Channel. This thick sheet was incredibly heavy, and one of the effects of the weight of ice was to carve out the underlying geology. As the ice gradually flowed from the Irish Sea basin south-east across the future Merseyside, it carved out parallel grooves from north-west to south-east. The largest of these was the channel of the Mersey itself, but the ice also created the valleys now holding the River Dee, the Fender on the Wirral and the River Alt and Ditton Brook on the east bank of the Mersey.

In very rare cases evidence has also been found which shows that the ice eradicated an earlier, slightly warmer period (known as an 'interglacial') when the

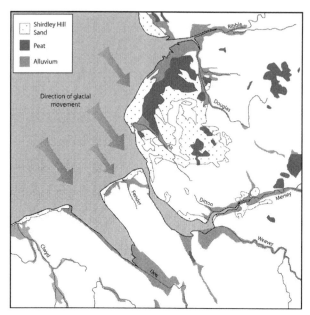

One of the earliest processes to influence the landscape, the ice sheet which flowed south from the Irish Sea basin carving out the Mersey, Dee, Weaver, Alt and other valleys. Today this results in a series of parallel grooves running north-west to south-east across the region, shaping everything from early human settlement to Liverpool's major west coastal position. (After Patmore, J.A. & Hodgkiss, A.G., *Merseyside in Maps*, p8, 1970, Longman, with additions)

area of Lancashire was covered in pine, spruce and birch. There have even been finds of hippopotamus and hyena in caves on the edge of the Pennines. These animal remains suggest that Lancashire had seen much warmer periods before the coming of the Ice Age.

Surface geology

Over the top of these geological layers, ground bare by the ice, we find wind-blown sand, known as Shirdley Hill Sand, which makes up the dunes found along the coast from Crosby to Southport. These were also first laid down as the ice retreated, and can form features up to 15m (49ft) tall around Little Crosby and Ince Blundell, while sand forms the base of hills up to 75m (246ft) further inland in the east of the county. Some of the sand in the area has been found to contain thin layers of organic material, demonstrating that conditions changed over time, switching between wind-blown sand depositions and temporary lakes where the organic material was laid on the lake-bed.

The most recent processes were the laying down of peat, clay and silt which formed damp, boggy moorland in hollows and low-lying areas, mostly in the north and west of the county, and near the Shirdley Sand hills. The two largest areas of this are the Simonswood and Chat Mosses, and these dictated the type of wildlife which lived in the area, as well as later settlement.

The shape of Merseyside

Due to this surface geology the lie of the land in Liverpool is one of rising and falling ridges as you move from the edge of the city, near Croxteth and Kirkby, past West Derby, Queens Drive, Tuebrook and Edge Hill. Some of the other higher areas of the region are remnants of this differing erosion; Mossley Hill/ Woolton, Everton Brow, Castle Street and Wallasey/Bidston were eroded less as the ice passed over them. Waves of high and low ground can also be traced inland from the Mersey to the north-east between Parbold and Billinge, each valley's direction reflecting the original course of the glacial flow.

So, the building blocks of Merseyside are the Triassic sandstone layers on which the city, and a large area around it, sit. Beyond this flat area the Carboniferous slopes of the Pennines and Snowdonia have formed a backdrop for millennia. The ice came later and helped carve out the Mersey, Dee and other smaller rivers in the area, but this uneven weathering left higher ground in ridges running parallel to the Mersey. As we shall see, all these processes, large and small, affected the manner in which Merseyside was first inhabited as the ice sheets gradually retreated. Thus the foundations of Merseyside were shaped before humans settled and began to alter the environment for their own ends.

THE EARLIEST PREHISTORY OF MERSEYSIDE – THE MESOLITHIC
The first traces of humans arriving on the banks of the Mersey come only after the ice retreated. Therefore, whereas many other parts of the United Kingdom have thrown up evidence of human activity up to 500,000 years old (from the Palaeolithic, or Old Stone Age), the remains of the activity of people in the Liverpool area can only be seen in the more recent Mesolithic, or middle Stone Age, around 10,000 years ago.

Movement and settlement
The sea level around this time was around 20m (66ft) lower than it is today. This means that dry land stretched out much further than it does now, with the coastline running from just west of Anglesey to west of Walney Island in Morecambe Bay. A band of now-submerged land around 10-15km (6-9 miles) wide lay between that line and the present coast.

This area was inhabited by small bands of people who moved between residential sites, with smaller locations associated with specialist hunting and gathering activities. These people must have only been seasonal occupants of the land, with a very mobile lifestyle. No evidence has been found for any buildings, but sites at Irby, Tarbock, Crosby and Lathom have revealed toolmaking evidence in the form of microliths – tiny stone tools used as weapons and knives. Ditton Brook was an important location also, and Mesolithic flint tool evidence points to this area being the location of repeated visits by Mesolithic humans. Their tools have been found either on the surface of the boggy layers, or eroding out of the stream bank, and this settlement may have been contemporary with that at Brunt Boggart, where similar evidence for Mesolithic occupation has been found. The pattern which emerges is that of camps along the Sefton and Mersey coast, some of them larger bases from which small groups would move out from. These small groups

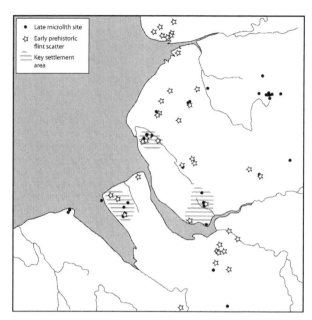

Some of the earliest evidence we have for human settlement comes from the Mesolithic era (around 5,000 years ago). There were no permanent settlements – instead, people moved between camps, possibly seasonally, to take advantage of different resources. Archaeological excavations may suggest favoured places which were repeatedly used. (After Cowell, R., 2010, Fig. 16, in *Journal of the Merseyside Archaeological Society* vol. 13, with additions)

would form camps where specific activities were carried out, such as toolmaking, foraging or butchery.

Another centre of activity is the mid-Wirral sandstone ridge. This is one of the ridges less eroded by the ice as it flowed south across the region and was probably drier and better drained than other parts of the peninsula. It was also more suitable for the favoured animals and plants which were hunted and foraged by these early human communities.

The best Mesolithic site in the region is at Greasby, Thursaston. Here the density of finds is at its highest in the county, with over 200 square metres covered in the remains of the flint toolmaking process. Not far away, at Greasby Copse, excavation revealed stone-lined pits (their function uncertain), and fragments of chert, which was the material used to make stone tools. The chert was shown through analysis to have come from North Wales, so even at this early stage, fairly long distance trade was essential for survival in this flint-poor area. The two sites at Tarbock – Ditton Brook and Ochre Brook – produced groups of stone tools between 50 and 250 pieces, and an excavation at Croxteth Park brought up another 500.

Although archaeological evidence for Mesolithic hunter-gatherers has been found around Merseyside, it is only in the later part of the period that we find clues to the activities of people close to what is now the city of Liverpool. Around 7,000 years ago, as the wetlands in the north-west were spreading and expanding, the earliest direct evidence for human occupation near Liverpool was created on the shores at Formby. Here, preserved in ancient sand layers, are sets of human footprints alongside those of deer, showing that humans were using the zone between high and low tides to hunt large animals.

Tools are some of the most common remains of Mesolithic culture. Known as 'microliths' these small (less than 10cm) stone flakes were fitted to shafts as arrow heads, or used on their own as scraping or cutting tools. These tools were discovered during an excavation at Croxteth Park. (Trustees of National Museums Liverpool)

A woodland landscape

The Mesolithic landscape was covered in forest up to 500m (1640ft) above sea level, consisting of oak, hazel, lime and elm. Just behind the coastal zones, and in the poorly drained hollows of the inlands and uplands, fens developed. The remains of these wetter areas give us small clues that humans were active in the area at this time. The surfaces of these boggy mires show evidence of burning, suggesting that perhaps the mixed woodland was being cleared deliberately, before being allowed to grow back. Bidston is an area where clearances look to have been at their greatest. While some of the fires would have been natural, humans would have been able to encourage an increase in the diversity of wildlife in the woodlands through partial clearance of small areas.

In general, the landscape at this time consisted of broken woodlands of oak and hazel, with patches of wetland, and the region was subject to frequent flooding. The land immediately on either side of the river would have been slightly more open, with a mixture of oak, hazel, alder, elm and pine, as well as shorter shrub-like vegetation taking advantage of the increased sunlight of the open land near the water. By 5000 BC, however, most of the land around the banks of the Mersey would have become mixed deciduous woodland, with the bogs and mosses mentioned previously breaking up the tree cover in places, in addition to the small areas cleared by humans.

Gathering food

The people here could rely on the well-stocked river, and the birds and plants inhabiting the banks, for food. There is also evidence for the killing of larger animals – wild pig and deer. The tidal Mersey would have encouraged a wide variety of animals for people to exploit, and the streams would have provided a route into the interior of the county before widespread clearance of woodland took place. The streams would also have provided the clean water needed for living, freshwater fish from the streams as well as saltwater fish from the Mersey estuary itself.

There are several sets of prehistoric footprints preserved in the Formby sands north of Liverpool. The earliest are Mesolithic, and give a startlingly vivid portrayal of a moment in time when humans crossed the beach here. Animal footprints have also been found, demonstrating that humans and wild animals existed in close proximity to each other. (Dave McAleavy Images)

The coastal lands, particularly sites at the mouths of the Ditton and the Alt and at Banks near Southport, have proven rich with Mesolithic material. As well as the variety of fish mentioned above, these areas had small amounts of flint washed up from the Irish Sea bed. It follows that areas near the mouth of the Mersey would have been important centres of population at this time, but these sites, if they existed, have been lost in the expansion of the city.

One of the classic signs of the change from the Mesolithic to the Neolithic is the emergence of farming. However, this distinction is no longer seen as black and white, and pollen evidence found in the Merseyside region shows that cereal-like plants were growing in what we might term the Mesolithic. Although the term 'cereal-like' doesn't necessarily indicate farming as we would recognise it today, it does show that by the end of the Mesolithic new technologies were slowly being adopted. However, other parts of the farming 'package' – farming, pottery and permanent settlement – were not yet taken up. Coastal locations, such as Flea Moss Wood in Little Crosby, Martin Mere and Hillhouse, have produced such plant evidence. It may be that connections with other communities around the Irish Sea and even down the Atlantic seaboard, which became so important in later prehistory, were already influencing life on the banks of the Mersey.

One thing we know very little about is the range of ritual beliefs and activities of these people. There is evidence on the European mainland of burial rituals as far back as 225,000 years ago, and it may be that the much more recent Mesolithic communities of Merseyside were performing similar activities, but none have left any traces for us to find today.

A 'NEW' STONE AGE?

Just as Mesolithic sites show signs of farming, an activity normally assigned to the Neolithic, so the early part of the Neolithic shows some continuity with the era before it. It was once stated that the Neolithic ('New Stone Age') brought with it farming, settlement, pottery and larger, much higher quality stone tools. This 'Neolithic package' was said to have come across from Europe with invaders or immigrants, along with the idea of building large stone monuments like the Calderstones and its associated burial practices. However, this process is now recognised as having been much more subtle, gradual and varied geographically.

On Merseyside people continued to be largely mobile. It might even have been the case that some groups carried on their lifestyle of moving from camp to camp (Neolithic structures have been excavated at Tatton Park), while others were already building houses and settling down. Excavations on the site of Beeston Castle in Cheshire have been dated to the early Neolithic, but many finds excavated there have a distinctly Mesolithic look to them. What the region lacks are the large, enclosed communal upland sites (called 'causewayed enclosures') which are so common in the south of England. This is partly a result of the landscape – there are few suitable locations on Merseyside for a hilltop settlement – and so it may be that smaller stone monuments may have acted as focal points where people would have come, from across the region, to assemble, trade and swap stories. These gatherings may have helped to give the earliest Merseysiders their identities, as well as the chance to gain tools and information to help them in their day-to-day lives. Many of these sites will have been lost to development, although a few are covered in this section.

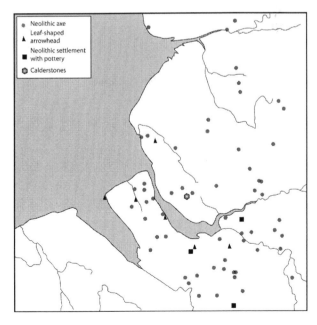

Compared to some parts of the country, there was little visible difference between the Mesolithic and Neolithic landscape. River mouths and the coast were still popular places to camp, life was still mostly mobile, and tool technology had not changed from the Mesolithic. (After Cowell, R., 2010, Fig. 16, in *Journal of the Merseyside Archaeological Society* vol. 13, with additions)

Stone for toolmaking – flint and chert

One of the main problems that prehistoric Liverpudlians had to contend with was the lack of local flint. The nearest sources for this essential Stone Age raw material were in Yorkshire, Wales, the Lake District and County Antrim in Ireland. Some small pebbles were probably to be found on the shores of the Irish Sea, washed up from the sea-bed, but not in sufficient quantity as a basis for making a living with. Unfortunately, archaeologists are not sure which of the other sources prehistoric people living on Merseyside got their flint from. It is suggested that it came mostly from the east, from Yorkshire and Derbyshire. For such stone to reach the banks of the Mersey, local communities may have been trading with the people of the Pennines, but it is also possible (perhaps even more likely) that raw material and finished tools travelled more indirectly, passing through the hands of many different owners until eventually they happened to reach the Mersey. As has been said already, many of these tools look similar to those which were created in the Mesolithic, and so local production of tools, using locally found flint, must have continued into the Neolithic.

Woodland clearance and the beginnings of farming

The landscape in which these people moved was at this time beginning to be cleared of trees. Small permanent gaps were appearing in the woodland, more often around the coast and in the central mosslands of south Lancashire than in the rest of the county. Such clearance allowed the bogs and mosses to increase in size, but would also have made the movements of game animals more predictable, aiding hunting.

Pollen evidence shows that farming was becoming more common around 4000 BC, replacing a landscape of open grasslands which had in turn developed in the wake of woodland clearances. People were clearing the forest to give themselves some room to grow the first cultivated cereals. Although this would have been nothing like the vast and dense crop we see across Britain today, these people would have helped plants spread and multiply, in order to gain the advantages of a more reliable food supply than nature would offer alone. Both upland and lowland areas were cleared of their woodland for this reason, from the coastal zone to the higher limestone areas. Knowsley Hall and Park today stand on land first cleared almost 5,000 years ago, and a similar process was occurring right across Britain, including land now covered by the Irish Sea.

However, there is relatively little cereal pollen evidence, so it may be that animal husbandry and hunting was more important. The remains of aurochs (wild ancestors of cattle) as well as red deer have been found in the region pointing to this possibility, and it has been suggested that good-quality livestock may have been the main indicator of wealth in the Neolithic.

Prehistoric religion

The Neolithic period is famous across Britain for the emergence of mega-lithic monuments. Stonehenge and Avebury are two of the more spectacular, and famous, but thousands dot the British landscape. These monuments give an insight into the world-view of the people who inhabited the region, as the monuments would have reflected their views of life after death, as well as something of the differentiation between members of the society – not everyone was buried in a chamber.

The major evidence of this type in Liverpool are the Calderstones, six meg-aliths which now stand in a greenhouse in the park which shares their name, and which was once part of the Harthill estate. Unfortunately the stones were removed from their original position in the nineteenth century, to be enclosed by the small wall on the roundabout at the bottom of Druids Cross Road which still stands today. Archaeologically speaking, this is a problem because those studying such monuments have found the landscape setting to be important in decoding

Above Although its function is still a matter for debate, the Calderstones would have taken the form of a mound with a passage from one side leading into the centre, similar to the Anglesey tomb of Bryn Celli Ddu, photographed here. The painting on the left shows the stones in their original position, probably around 20m west of the roundabout at the south end of Druids Cross Road. (Liverpool Record Office, Liverpool Libraries; tpholland, Creative Commons Attribution 2.0 Generic (CC BY 2.0))

Left The Calderstones are covered in carvings of spirals, cups, circles and other shapes. It's been suggested that these remains are some of the most decorated of their kind, and may also have been some of the latest. If those who used the tomb were some of the last of their kind, perhaps they sought to preserve themselves through the elaboration of their tombs. The carved artwork we see today may have been hidden inside, for only the 'initiated' to see during ceremonies. (Aerial-Cam (AS-GN) / MAS 2007) their meaning. As no other Neolithic landmarks have made it down to our era, this is a double problem for someone trying to piece together the motivations behind the builders.

Fortunately, evidence from the carvings on the stones, as well as comparisons with other Neolithic monuments, tells us some important details about not only the funerary practices of the Neolithic Merseysiders, but also about important factors in their day-to-day lives. The closest relatives to the Calderstones are the well-preserved passage tombs of south-west Scotland, Ireland, North Wales and Cornwall. The two best preserved are Barclodiad y Gawres and Bryn Celli Ddu in North Wales, and the original Calderstones monument would have looked just like them.

The Calderstones have been described as some of the most decorated mega-lithic stones in mainland Britain, and this decoration has parallels with the Irish tombs of Newgrange, Knowth and Dowth, as well as art in the aforementioned Welsh tombs. One of the daggers from the Calderstones in fact has parallels with a dagger seen on a monument in Campo Lamerio Valley, Galicia, Spain. There is a suggestion that the passage grave tradition began in Iberia, and spread north along the Atlantic coast to Brittany, Cornwall, Wales, Ireland and Merseyside. And so we can begin to see that the spheres of communication, seen in earlier millennia to extend as far as Wales and Derbyshire, must have been widening in the Neolithic.

On a more local scale, the Neolithic landscape of Liverpool contained other monuments now lost. A map of 1568, produced as part of a boundary dispute between Allerton and Wavertree, shows three additional monuments, only one of which still stands. The Calderstones themselves (described as three standing stones) sat on the boundary, were used as a marker and therefore important in this argument. Another large monument is the 'Pikeloo Hill', standing to the south-

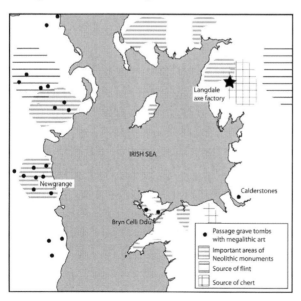

Langdale axe factory

IRISH SEA

Newgrange

Calderstones

Bryn Celli Ddu

● Passage grave tombs with megalithic art

Important areas of Neolithic monuments

Source of flint

Source of chert

By noting comparisons with tombs of a similar age around the Irish Sea, we can use the Calderstones' cousins to suggest what the monument would have looked like when it was completed. It is thought that a large number of tombs of similar age and style, found all around the Irish Sea zone, prove that cultural links existed between the communities which built them.

west of the Calderstones. This may have been a passage tomb like the surviving monument, or possibly a later Bronze Age barrow, like those green mounds which are so common in the Peak District and south-west Britain today. The second monument was the 'Rodger Stone'. This monolith may have been originally part of the Caldertones or the Pikeloo Hill, or possibly a menhir – such isolated megaliths can be seen in south-west British, Irish and north French landscapes today. The third monument, and one which survivs today, albeit in a new location, is the 'Robin Hood Stone'. Like the Rodger Stone it may have originally been incorporated in a larger monument, or been a menhir in its own right. The Robin Hood Stone has rock art similar to that of the Calderstones on the faces of its buried section, suggestive of a very old tradition. It may be that this monument was already old when the Calderstones were erected, and was incorporated into a Neolithic 'ritual landscape' when other monuments emerged.

These monuments were singled out in the boundary dispute in which they were important, but it may be that other Neolithic (and Bronze Age) landmarks originally existed but have not lasted into the modern era. There are records of Neolithic stone tool and pottery finds from Wavertree and Allerton, but little other evidence to tell us about the rest of the landscape.

Analysis of the placing of these monuments (where this can be identified for certain) suggests further parallels with similar monuments elsewhere. The Caldertones (which probably orignally stood around 20m to the west of their roundabout location) are part-way up a hillside, rather than being at the top or in a valley. The Robin Hood Stone, and possibly the Rodger Stone, were lower down in the valley. It has been suggested that the isolated menhirs were on routeways in the valley bottom, while the burial chambers were on higher ground, away from routinely used land such as farmland. The menhirs may have

Prehistoric monuments remained important long after their original use had been forgotten. By 1568 the stones were used as part of the township boundary between Allerton and Childwall, and so when a dispute arose this map was produced, which shows that the Calderstones were not the only possible prehistoric monuments in the area. Also marked are the Pikeloo Hill, possibly another tomb or an even larger mound, as well as the Rodger Stone, now disappeared, and the Robin Hood Stone, which still stands in Allerton, though a slight distance from its original position. (Liverpool Record Office, Liverpool Libraries)

been waymarkers on routes used when formally approaching the Calderstones during funerary and other rituals. While it is difficult to extrapolate this information to suggest the existence of other monuments, for Neolithic people the landscape would have been populated with reminders of the religious side of life, with the cultivated lowlands containing pointers to the monuments which sat in clearings in the wooded uplands.

The style and placing of the monuments shows that there were cultural connections of some kind across the Irish Sea and beyond, and it may have been that these connections were more important than those inland (to the Pennines, Cheshire and the Lake District), where other evidence for Neolithic activity has been found. The Calderstones themselves show art styles suggestive of a great length of time in use, perhaps as long as 800 years from the Neolithic to the middle or late Bronze Age. It may even be the case that the Calderstones was one of the last monuments of its kind, before other traditions took over in the Bronze Age. The poor survival of these monuments hides the fact that they were important for such a long time, and drew on connections across great distances.

THE BRONZE AGE ON MERSEYSIDE

Towards the end of the Neolithic and into the Bronze Age, the climate began to deteriorate. Woodland returned to many areas as the region experienced wetter conditions around 4,500 years ago, and mossy bogs appeared in places such as Leasowe Bay on the Wirral. Sea levels had not stopped moving, and by the end of the Neolithic it was 8m (26ft) above what it is today. The land slopes westwards

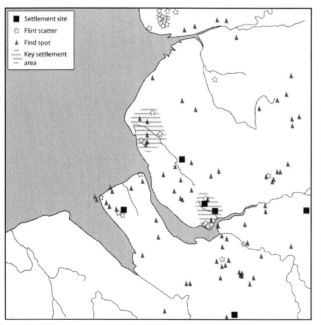

Although not as prominent as in other parts of Britain at this time, settlements and farmsteads appear in the archaeological record during the Bronze Age. People still travelled to take advantage of different natural resources, however, using the higher ground inland during wetter parts of the year, and the coastal plain when it was warmer. (After Cowell, R., 2010, Fig. 18, in *Journal of the Merseyside Archaeological Society* vol. 13, with additions)

only slowly, so shingle ridges formed in the shallow seas. Some of these can now be identified up to 1km (0.6 miles) inland, left as the sea level fell in later eras.

Settlements and farming

Although a settled way of life was becoming more important across Britain, communities in the north-west remained partly mobile. Evidence suggests that Bronze Age groups would have exploited the lowlands only seasonally, probably in the summer, while retreating to the drier uplands for the wetter parts of the year. Although farmsteads are minor elements in the archaeological record from this time, small-scale farming did occur in the Bronze Age, shown by pollen evidence from Mount Pleasant, Waterloo, dating to around 3,000 years ago. Large areas of woodland were cleared at this time, such as at Simonswood and Parr Moss, strengthening the suggestion that people were involved in agriculture.

Marking Merseyside and Cheshire out from other regions of Bronze Age Britain, however, there is less evidence for absolutely permanent settlement by the inhabitants. It is possible that people, as well as moving from season to season, paused in some locations for a few years at a time. The single buildings which have been found may have been used for dwellings, or they may have been simple agricultural buildings.

Despite their rarity, there are a handful of settlements which have been excavated on Merseyside. Irby, on the Wirral, revealed traces of cereal cultivation, metalworking and textile production from the middle Bronze Age, and at Tarbock archaeologists found a short section of a ditch containing characteristic early Bronze Age pots, known as Beakers. In Kirkby a semi-circular structure associated with Bronze Age pottery was excavated, while at Brunt Boggart a deposit of stones and burnt material was found, and has been compared to the burnt mounds (used possibly for cooking, or industrial processes) found at this time in various parts of Britain and Ireland.

Outside Merseyside, settlements have been found at Manchester Airport, and also the Pennines. Some of these settlements appear to have lasted much longer than their western neighbours, and it has been suggested that these were higher status sites. Perhaps prehistoric Liverpudlians were part of a wider network of contacts who travelled to the Pennines, like they had in the Neoithic, to trade, gossip and feast.

The later phases of footprints found on the Formby shoreline are from the Bronze Age. Coupled with the evidence for dogs, aurochs, red deer, boar and horse found on the north Wirral coast, it is clear that this was still an era of mobile pastoralists. What is likely is that land use differed with location, so that some areas were settled more or less permanently, and farmed, while elsewhere in the landscape there were small camps used for specific jobs, such as toolmaking or butchery. The poorer conditions may have meant that cereal farming was more difficult, while animal farming was carried out on the drier uplands further inland.

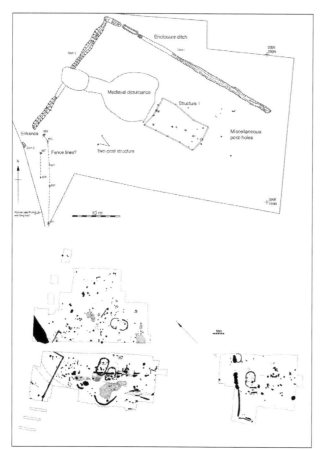

These structures excavated in south Liverpool in the last two decades show that buildings were almost oval in shape. The buildings – constructed of wood, clay and thatch – stood within enclosures, which were a developing characteristic of the Bronze and Iron Ages in this part of the country (see main text for further detail). (Trustees of National Museums Liverpool)

Tools – stone and bronze

Bronze Age communities still made common use of stone tools, and scatters of stone-working debris have been excavated at Hale, Irby and Little Crosby. Middens – large mounds of discarded food, pottery and bones – found on the north Wirral coast were probably created by the same communities who made these late stone tools. Like those of previous periods, tools from the Bronze Age are often difficult to tell from tools of the end of the Neolithic, and there was certainly continuity in tool styles. Excavations at Little Crosby discovered the remains of stone tools production, with little waste. This is further evidence of local collection of raw material, with the toolmakers present at small, temporary camps for the express purpose of collecting and knapping flint.

For a period popularly known as the Bronze Age, there is very little evidence on Merseyside for metal production at this time. There have been discoveries of metal hoards however (at Portfield Camp, Whalley and Winmarleigh) and such finds reveal that these objects did exist in the wider region. There are also extensive copper mines along the North Wales coast, at Parys Mountain on Anglesey and Great Orme at Llandudno, which would have provided plenty of raw material for copper smelting. The late Bronze Age layers at Irby depict a settlement with some evidence of metalworking, although the settlements at Little Crosby and Hale are dominated by stone tool debris rather than metalwork.

Bronze Age burials

Records tell us that prehistoric ceramic urns have been found at sites across Merseyside, such as at West Kirby and Wavertree, in recent centuries. Although the Wavertree finds did not have a mound associated with them, urns are closely associated with Bronze Age burial practices (and in fact the mound may simply have been destroyed at some point). Urns and bones are also known to have come from the half-flattened mound in which the Calderstones once stood. The carved feet on the stones themselves also have parallels with known Bronze Age monuments elsewhere in the country, and so we can safely say that the Calderstones were still in use, and being altered, into the Bronze Age. The specific landscape context of the monument may have changed, but the local inhabitants would have been incorporating the stones into their own religion.

THE IRON AGE

The woodland clearance that we saw begin as a patchwork in the Mesolithic was probably widespread across north-west England by the Iron Age, and use of the land had intensified by this point. Marshy areas were still common, and temperatures were falling while rainfall increased. This reduced the space available for grazing animals and cultivating cereals, although the coast would have been relatively warmer.

Evidence for growing crops is not as extensive as that for farming animals, at least until the end of the Iron Age. The proximity to the coast meant more frost-free days than for those further inland, and with Wales acting as a rain-shadow the Wirral and west Lancashire would have been a good place to cultivate crops. There is pollen evidence from Irby and Beeston Castle for bread wheat, barley and oats, but on the east bank of the Mersey the site of Brook House Farm, in Halewood, is more dominated by butchery and cooking evidence, such as cattle and pig bones. There are few clues to the field system in use, but the first farmsteads in the region come from this period, and so it's likely that the Merseyside landscape included small enclosed fields similar to those found in Cheshire. Only Brook House Farm has provided any plant remains or animal bones north of the Mersey (though grain storage structures were found at Lathom), so archaeologists clearly have a lot still to learn about this stage in Liverpool's history.

Hill forts and enclosures

Impressive multiple-ditched hill forts are a common feature of the Iron Age landscape around Britain, and the wider Liverpool hinterland has its share, such as near Frodsham, Eddisbury, Kelsbarrow and at Beeston in Cheshire. However, the

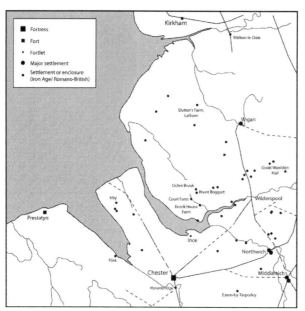

This map demonstrates something of the peripheral nature of Merseyside during the so-called Romano-British period. Roman roads bypassed the future Liverpool, travelling from Chester to Carlisle via Warrington. Another road is believed to stretch from the north gate of Chester to Meols on the north Wirral coast. However, despite the lack of Roman contact, Merseyside has thrown up some evidence of settlement activity during the Iron Age. (After Cowell, R., 2010, Fig. 18, in *Journal of the Merseyside Archaeological Society* vol. 13, with additions)

lack of uplands in Liverpool itself prevented the creation of these landmarks, and so the enclosures at Mill Hill Road, Irby, and at Woolton and Brook House Farm, Halewood, may have acted as a replacement, and they share features in common.

The suggestion is that the upland hill forts were something of a higher status site, which those people in the lowlands looked to for larger gatherings as well as protection. However, just as the presence of hill forts has been used as evidence for a hierarchy, so the lack of such sites on Merseyside has been seen as a lack of hierarchy, and the presence of a more egalitarian society. The tribes in the area were the Brigantes and the Cornovii, but the extent to which these people lived in harmony (or even saw themselves as sharing one identity) is in dispute. Perhaps the Iron Age communities of Merseyside were somewhat isolated from the rest of Lancashire and Cheshire, still looking to their friends across and around the Irish Sea, and had little need for larger defended sites like Beeston. In any case, the settlements in the lowlands of the Mersey estuary would have been small and scattered, and so would have been vulnerable in the case of inter-tribal conflict should it arise.

It has been suggested that Iron Age wealth was shown off not through belongings, precious metals or weapons, but rather through the breeding and large-scale consumption of cattle. The arrangement of ditches and entrances at Brook House Farm would support this idea, as they would have been suitable for corralling these animals. Also, despite not being set on a hilltop like Beeston, the farm could have been a site of high status not just for its cattle herds but because of the physical size of the place.

The farm was most likely situated in a clearing, as pollen evidence suggests that heavy woodland surrounded it in the Iron Age. Towards the end of the Iron Age, however, this situation was changing, and cattle enclosures in the region become smaller. It is possible that cereal cultivation was becoming more important again, or could mean that cattle corralling was no longer a communal activity, each of the later enclosures being designed for only one family's livestock.

Trading beyond Merseyside

Wirral may have been on the edge of society, away from the Iron Age centres of power in Shropshire and Lancashire, but Cheshire salt was already becoming a valuable commodity, traded over the north-west of England, Wales and the Midlands. As the Iron Age progressed, and we come to the end of the prehistoric period, Carthaginian coins and Roman amphorae (from the south coast of France) found their way to Meols, an important beach site 'emporium' at the north end of the Wirral. Glass beads produced by a method developed on the Continent have also been found. All these things show the very widespread trade which was going on, with links between Merseyside and mainland Europe and the Mediterranean, as well as more local links. Merseyside was in contact with the Romans, and almost all Iron Age sites produce some Roman artefacts, but much of the wider region was only slowly Romanised compared to some parts of the country.

THE ROMANS IN NORTH-WEST ENGLAND

The term 'Romano-British' suits the balance of native and Roman culture seen in the region around 2,000 years ago. Although the Roman armies built a road between Chester, Warrington and Carlisle, any influence of Roman culture on pre-existing British communities to the west of this route is hard to see in the archaeological record. A Romano-British burial was found at Leasowe on the Wirral, and metal detecting has found scatters of coins and brooches across Merseyside, but more substantial traces like the buildings expected at Romano-British period sites like Meols have likely been eroded by the sea. Some Roman artefacts did make their way up the Wirral and to where Liverpool itself now stands, but more Romanisation than this is doubtful.

Aerial photography and reconnaissance has brought to light many more sites in recent years, although its strength lies naturally in rural areas. Nevertheless, it seems that the landscape of Roman-era Merseyside contained a mixture of enclosures, farms and homesteads. The second half of the Iron Age had seen the disappearance of communal sites and large cattle corralling features, and as a result the Romano-British landscape shows only smaller-scale settlement.

There was a settlement at Ochre Brook, Tarbock, which had been occupied since prehistory, but even once the Romans had made inroads into the rest of the country, only selected parts of their culture made it into the Ochre Brook area (e.g. there are no villas known from Merseyside). The farm here cultivated barley, and there was certainly hay and grassland, and the buildings were oval or rectangular. It is also possible that the inhabitants exploited the small amount of coal which was exposed in the banks of the brook itself. The site at Court Farm, Halewood, shows evidence of occupation from the second to the fourth century in an unenclosed settlement with up to a dozen rectangular structures, and field ditches.

The clearance of woodland, and the increase in crop farming and field-creation continued into the period. Settlements, which were becoming more permanent, would have been separated by belts of woodland, scrub wasteland and the ever-present marshes. The extent of the field systems was still a lot smaller than similar features known from places like Nottinghamshire and Yorkshire, however. The landscape may have been one of arable farms in oval ditched enclosures, some of which were still visible when the early Ordnance Survey maps were published (although their date is uncertain). Both enclosed and unenclosed settlements were present along the banks of the 'Seteia' (Mersey), some with histories stretching back into the Iron Age, and connected with trackways amongst the field systems in the landscape. Most enclosures were still being created along stream channels (the Bollin, Weaver and Glaze Brook), which would have provided easier routes to transport locally sourced materials such as coal, iron and lead. The materials would have found a market in Roman Chester (Deva), and have been excavated at the sites of Ochre Brook and Court Farm, where coal in particular was used for iron smithing, copper alloy working and domestic heating.

Trade and contact

Meols continued to be an important emporium, and there is speculation that the road from the north gate of Chester led up the Wirral to Meols. Victorian and earlier antiquarians collected vast numbers of finds from the shore, not only from Roman times but also the medieval period which followed. Meols was of sufficient size to maintain its importance for an extended period and so, despite a generally poor amount of Roman finds on Merseyside, it is very likely that Meols and the wider region engaged in trade with the invading army.

The Roman army was a resource-hungry enterprise, and brought with it a support network of record-keepers, traders, farmers and families. Cheshire and Lancashire would have taken advantage of this opportunity, supplying the Roman towns and forts, and would even have been encouraged (or coerced) by the Romans themselves who were keen on exploiting under-used areas. The routes via Warrington to towns further north (such as Carlisle), not to mention the garrisons on Hadrian's Wall, would have allowed lowland north-west England to act as a supply zone to maintain the military machine. The Romans would, like King John later, have found north Wirral useful also as a launching point for offensives against North Wales and up the Lancashire coast. Even if contact was sporadic and short-lived, Merseyside would have been of some importance to the Romans.

Early industry on the banks of the Mersey

In addition to the use of coal where available, in the Romano-British period sand was being exploited at Whitefield Sandhole, and sandstone was quarried at Bank Hey Delf (south-east of Ochre Brook). Stone is known to have been quarried at Storeton on the Wirral, and this stone may have been used in inscriptions in Chester itself.

One of the intriguing aspects of industry at this time was the production of Roman tiles at Ochre Brook. Although no Roman coins have as yet been found in the immediate area, there is more evidence of Romanisation here than in any of the surrounding region. Stamps on the tiles themselves show that there were certainly links between the tile manufacturer and the Twentieth Roman Legion based in Chester. Pottery found on the site was locally made, with nothing quite the same being found anywhere else. There is some evidence that building style was influenced by Roman ideas, and it may be the case that whoever lived at Ochre Brook 2,000 years ago was a retired legionary. Perhaps this Roman had taken to producing tiles for the Roman army based in Chester while living out his retirement in his modest farmstead in the countryside!

Other industries were small-scale, including the smithing (though not smelting) of iron at Irby and Court Farm, as well as copper alloy production. Meols continued to be an important regional port, and Roman coins begin to appear here from the AD 50s and 60s, no doubt introduced through trade. Amphorae containing wine and oil have also been found, and these containers were used to transport their contents in bulk via boat. An undated boat was excavated from Tryon Street (part of the Pool which now lies under Queens Square) in 1932 which contained a number of Roman coins, but coin evidence shows that trade links stretched as far as Dorset in Britain and Marseilles on the Continent.

As in the Iron Age, it is possible to see Merseyside as being on the periphery of Roman 'civilisation'. It may have been a rural area where retired soldiers retreated to in their later years, and where raw materials were sourced before being taken to centres like Chester. British tribes still existed during the Roman occupation, ready and willing to trade with or fight the incomers, and so, despite the lack of archaeological finds, Merseyside is likely to have been both an important trading centre and a strategic coastal location.

MEDIEVAL MERSEYSIDE

By the beginning of the fifth century AD the Roman Empire was in disarray. The final garrisons left these shores during Constantine's reign, around AD 407. Left behind were the British (albeit with some inevitable mixing with the Roman incomers). Germanic tribes were migrating around mainland Europe at this time, contributing to Rome's fall, and they reached these shores in the following centuries. Later on in the Middle Ages the Danes and the Norse also made their way across the North Sea, settling in vast areas of eastern England and in Ireland.

Place name evidence tells us more about the medieval period on Merseyside than in any other period. We can map the extent of Viking settlement compared to British, and even tell some details about the nature of the settlement itself through the name. Landscape features, political centres and settlement types can all be indicated through these names.

The period between the end of the Roman presence in Britain and the Norman invasion of 1066 was one of a shifting balance of power in the British Isles. Danes moved west into Lancashire, and Vikings arrived on the banks of the Mersey in two waves, directly from Scandinavia and secondly following their expulsion from Dublin in AD 902.

Place names

There is very little archaeological evidence on Merseyside for the early medieval period. Our best source of evidence, given what we know about the British Isles as a whole during this time, is the place names of the towns and villages around the region. Domesday Book refers to over 450 places, although not all of them by name. Referring to Domesday and the modern map gives clues as to where the European invaders landed and set up their homes.

There are two groups of names on Merseyside in the period from the fifth to the eleventh centuries: British and Scandinavian. The Old English (British) names represent the population who were here by the time the Romans removed their garrisons from these shores, and include Bootle ('botl' – a dwelling place) and Walton ('wala tun' – a British farm), and these may be said to be the oldest place-names in the area. They may even have a history going back into the Roman or prehistoric periods.

The Scandinavian names include some drawn from the language of the incoming Danes and Norwegians: Toxteth ('Tocca's staith', or landing place), the Mersey ('maeres ea' – boundary river) and Kirkby ('Cherchebi' – village with a church). Irby – Irish settlement – tells the story of those Norse who were ejected from Dublin in AD 902 and came across to the Wirral, as opposed to the Danes who came direct from Scandinavia or migrated across the Pennines from landing places on the Yorkshire coast. Croxteth ('Krokr's Staith'), Speke ('spaec' – place near brushwood) and Knowsley ('Cēnwulfes lēah' – Cēnwulf's meadow) are further Norse names on the boundaries of the modern city.

A look at the distribution shows that Scandinavian place names occur more often on the River Alt and on the coast, with the Alt names surrounded by British ones. Scandinavian names often describe the location inhabited, such as Meols, meaning 'sandhills', and further analysis suggests that the 'invaders' were forced to live on whatever land was as yet uninhabited, and therefore of lower quality. This seems odd in light of the traditional view of Vikings as raiders and pillagers, but there are no records of violence associated with the Norsemens' arrival on Merseyside. There would inevitably have been skirmishes, but in this sparsely populated area any large-scale fighting seems to have been restricted to later in the period. The place name Raby ('boundary village') suggests a definite awareness of where the division between British and Scandinavian communities lay.

The Norse incomers were certainly no opportunistic invaders. Once here they had every intention of making permanent settlement, as proven by the existence of 'Thing' places. Thingwall in West Derby and on the Wirral would both have been the site of the Norse 'thing', or parliament (and the location of the former may have played a part in West Derby's rise to prominence in later centuries). The small rise on which Thingwall Hall sits today may even be the exact location of the local Thing.

Early medieval settlement and land use

There has always been the question of the age of medieval settlement on Merseyside, and to what extent there was continuity from the Romano-British period. From a landscape perspective, there does seem to be a similarity between the locations occupied in the Roman era and those inhabited by the medieval British (sites at Court Farm, Halewood, Mill Hill Road, Irby and Hoylake Road, Moreton on the Wirral) but it is not always easy to state that settlement was continuous. Later medieval buildings (tenth century) have been excavated which show that they were constructed on the filled-in ditches of previous buildings, but it could just be that the new buildings were taking advantage of the already flat land which the old buildings had prepared.

Whether or not Romano-British settlements were inhabited continuously through to the medieval period, it is certain that later Merseysiders rejuvenated villages that had seen some decline after the Romans left, dragging much of the economy with them. Meols on the north Wirral coast was one such settlement. Although much of the remains of this town are only visible at low tide, Meols, which had been a major regional Roman-era port, was clearly still a major centre of trade and exchange. Finds from the tenth and eleventh centuries even hint at the presence of a mint here, making imitations of other British coins. Finds from the shoreline include exotic goods indicating wide trading links,

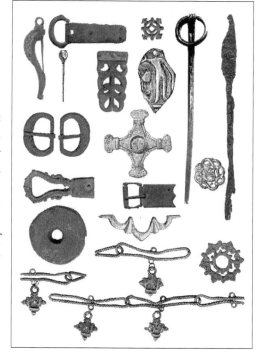

Meols was an important trading centre from the Iron Age onwards, and by the medieval period it had contacts as far afield as the Mediterranean. The array of finds in this photograph are just some of those found by chance over the past 200 years. (Trustees of National Museums Liverpool)

for example a pottery flask from St Menas in North Africa. Meols was to lose its importance to Chester later on, but as far as archaeology is concerned, medieval Meols has produced finds second only to London in terms of size and importance.

The Romans had made use of Meols as a jumping off point for defending themselves against the Welsh and Brigantes, and in the medieval period Merseyside continued to be a boundary area. To the north of the river in the seventh century was Northumbria, which was a huge kingdom stretching to the east coast of England and north to present-day Edinburgh. To the south and west of the Mersey was Mercia. A hoard of 350 gold coins hidden at Harkirk, Little Crosby, and discovered in 1611 shows that periods of unrest did occur. At the start of the tenth century all the land between the Ribble and Mersey came under English (Mercian) control under the leadership of Edward, King of Wessex. After 973 it was part of the king's own land (the 'royal demesne'), with the large township of West Derby, centred on the current village site, being part of the demesne too.

Villages, parishes and townships

Within these political systems the settlements of medieval Merseyside consisted of enclosures and farmsteads, such as those excavated at Hoylake Road on the Wirral and Court Farm in Halewood. An excavation at Telegraph Road, Irby revealed a farm on richer agricultural land, and so makes a stronger case for continuity from Romano-British times.

The kingdoms and townships were divided into manors, with a central manorial seat surrounded by farms. The manor of West Derby, as described in Domesday, would have had Liverpool as one of these manor farms, although it was not named in the survey. The manorial sites would often have been impressive moated houses, such as moated sites found at Speke, Kirkdale (Bank Hall) and St Helens (though only Speke in this case was manorial), sited away from nucleated settlement.

In general, the lands around south Lancashire were of relatively poor quality, and the landscape was sparsely populated, with large parishes and townships. There were perhaps around 7,000 or 8,000 people in the whole of Lancashire around AD 1000, with the nearest settlement to West Derby being Chester. The farms, in the landscape surrounding the manorial seats, were therefore widely disbursed; a mixture of arable and pastoral. It may be that this difference depended on whether the farm was in the uplands or lowlands, but at the moment the number of sites which have been analysed is too small to tell.

Open arable field systems are known to have existed in West Derby, Much and Little Woolton, Speke, Childwall and Fazakerley. This system was one where local farmers would each have a number of strips within a larger open field, rather than separate enclosed fields, and would rotate the crops each year in order to avoid exhausting the soil.

The open field areas were located around the outside of the royal hunting forest of Lancaster. Hunting forests were subject to strict development rules and were large areas of land (the one on Merseyside stretching from Toxteth to Simonswood) reserved for the king's hunt. Such strict land management forbade farming or development, and so open fields were more widespread in those areas outside the 'pale' – the enclosing boundary ditch and bank (topped with a fence) which kept game animals in and wild animals, and unauthorised humans, out.

Not all the forest would be wooded, and not all the woodland would be part of the royal forest. Therefore when population increased in the later medieval period (eleventh and thirteenth centuries) the edges of the woodland were eaten into to create new farmland. This 'assarting' is evident in Fazakerley and other areas on the edge of the forest. Pressure on farmland can also be inferred from the presence of ancient woodland revealed in eroding sand dunes – during the seventh and eighth centuries an increasingly stormy climate buried potential farmland under coastal wind-blown sand, and attempts were made to stabilise these hungry features by planting them with hardy marram and starr grasses. The mosses of Sefton were also eventually drained and converted to farmland as the demand for space grew.

Apart from farming, small-scale quarrying was carried out to supply building material, and such quarrying carried on over subsequent centuries, with field and road names revealing the former existence of this industry.

Medieval buildings

The buildings of the early farmsteads would have been wood-framed, perhaps resting on stone pads for their foundations. The walls were of clay and straw wattle and daub. The famous hogback stone of West Kirby, as well as others like it around Europe, were based on the distinctive house shape of medieval Denmark, complete with the shingles used to roof the houses. Houses have been excavated from Hoylake Road and Irby on the Wirral, as well as Tatton in Cheshire. The tenth- to twelfth-century Irby buildings were elliptical (bow sided), with a more sturdy, rock-cut foundation filled with clay, and some (along with the Tatton buildings) may have been a type of hall. Other buildings from this era have been excavated at Meols, Brunt Boggart and Fazakerley.

The churches of the time were also of wooden construction, but have all been succeeded by more recent stone-built buildings. The most likely oldest churches in the area were those at Huyton, Kirkby, Prescot, Walton and Childwall. The church at Kirkby is dedicated to St Chad, a seventh-century bishop of Lichfield (in which bishopric Kirkby sat). The churches of Walton, Childwall and Huyton have distinctive oval churchyards, which are characteristic of pre-Norman Conquest sites. Walton eventually became the mother church of the area, and monasteries were founded at Birkenhead, Stanlow (moved to Whalley in 1296), Burscough and Runcorn. There were also the remains of a fifteenth-century Moss Grange in Allerton until the twentieth century.

Politics and settlement at the Norman Conquest

The landscape was divided into hundreds. There are many theories as to what the exact definition of a hundred was, but suffice to say that it was a large land division, though varying in size, and that West Derby Hundred was the most important in this area. West Derby was a royal manor, in the demesne of Edward the Confessor, and probably included a fortified house and a hunting lodge.

West Derby in this sense occupied the vast majority of what was until recently south Lancashire, but the centre of power was the 'wapentake', a meeting of co-operative tribes, families or villages for purposes of defence. A wapentake court was held every three weeks in the presence of the steward of the hundred, where the largely self-governing communities swore allegiance. The courts of the lord of the manor – the Halmote – were also held at West Derby, for the manors of West Derby itself as well as the manors of Crosby and Wavertree.

West Derby is a classic example of a manorial seat: it sat at the entrance to the lord's estate, with the three other elements of social control – the chapel, court house and castle – close by. Barrett's Hall, the predecessor of Croxteth Hall, was built on the site of the chief forester's dwelling, although this has not been found. The castle was built around 1100 by Roger de Poitou, and the chapel sat in the centre of the village where the monument now stands. The courthouse is the Elizabethan successor to the venue holding the regional court (Portmoot). Domesday Book also records a hawk's eyrie, a hunting forest and a game reserve. This was certainly a place for nobility and kings to enjoy a pastime of hunting and sport.

The village, like many similar ones around Lancashire and Cheshire, had a central nucleus with roads leading out from it. Along the roads were houses with long gardens – crofts – stretching out behind them. These crofts are found along the 'town row' – in West Derby fossilised into the road name – with a 'back lane' (not coincidentally the former name of Eaton Road) bounding the rear side.

The strict forest law, which restricted the development of farming or building, was relaxed in the thirteenth century, spurring clearance and reducing the wood-

The land divisions of the later medieval period are better known than those of earlier times. Domesday Book is the most useful source for this, as it used these divisions to survey the tax returns for the country. The largest division in the area was the hundred of West Derby, which was part of Lancashire, and divided into parishes and townships. These divisions formed the basis for political control and the operating of local courts.

land cover. Population was growing in the first half of the fourteenth century, but a series of poor harvests, social unrest and animal diseases halted this expansion. Climatic changes were reducing the available farmland, and when the bubonic plague reduced the population by up to a third a shift was made from arable to pastoral farming, which took fewer people to operate.

As the woodland was eaten into in order to create new land for building, this assarting led to the expansion of West Derby away from the village centre and out towards Knotty Ash in the south and Norris Green in the north. The frequency of the name 'Green' in the area (Norris, Almonds, Haymans), 'ley' ('clearing' – as found in Leyfield) and 'hey' ('enclosure', as in Alder Hey and Kiln Hey) attest to the wooded nature of the manor, and the process of reclaiming wooded land which must have occurred.

The importance of this settlement can be gauged by the presence of up to three mills (a windmill, horsemill and a watermill). These were heavily protected resources, and their presence near the centre of regional power is not surprising. West Derby Castle was garrisoned with troops at the time of Liverpool's founding, and the village and hundred were at the centre of power for a large region around. It may seem odd for John to have chosen the empty and unimportant berewick of Liverpool over the natural centre of West Derby, but it is clear that the king wished to lay the foundations of his new town in virgin territory, and keep control for himself.

MERSEYSIDE AT LIVERPOOL'S FOUNDATION

By the start of the thirteenth century Merseyside was a sparsely populated area with a few nucleated settlements. Surrounding the manorial centres were the scattered farms (manors) of which Liverpool was one. European unrest had led to communities coming together under strong lords for protection, and the medieval feudal system was born. This had not penetrated too much into Britain, but when William the Conqueror arrived from France he imposed it wholesale across the country. The essence of the system was that the whole of the land belonged ultimately to the king, being passed out as rewards to his loyal lords. Roger of Poitou was lucky enough to have been given West Derby in this way for his part in the Conquest of 1066, and the village remained the centre of local governance for centuries after this.

However, the banks of the Mersey remained – as the name suggested – a boundary area, perhaps even a no man's land of poor farming and boggy mosslands. It was not until 1199 when John succeeded his brother Richard as King of England that a change in this status appeared on the horizon. John had failed appallingly when trusted to rule Ireland on behalf of his brother. Perhaps seeking to redeem himself he once again cast his eyes across the Irish Sea. The lands which had once belonged to Poitou had eventually been granted to one Warine of Lancaster by Henry II (John's and Richard's father). Warine's son Henry had inherited it, but John identified Liverpool's strategic position as an undeveloped area near the coast. Giving Henry the manor of English Lea in return, John took Liverpool into his possession, and on 28 August 1207 signed a charter creating the borough of 'Liverpul', and giving anyone holding a burgage 'all liberties and free customs … which any free borough on the sea has in our land'. The story of Liverpool as a sparsely populated backwater was coming to an end.

CHAPTER 2

FROM LIVERPOOL'S FOUNDATION TO THE CIVIL WAR

King John signed letters patent (a public proclamation) on 24 August 1207, calling all who would take burgages – rented building plots – in the town to come to Liverpool, and enjoy all the freedoms from customs and market taxes as was usually granted in any of the king's boroughs.

But before John ever considered a new town on this part of the north-west coast, south-west Lancashire had an existing complex system of ownership and rule. Although Liverpool had rarely been mentioned by name before John's charter, there must have been an existing settlement, even if only a handful of meagre houses or a manorial farm belonging to West Derby.

THE NATURAL LANDSCAPE

A look at the lie of the land, when Liverpool was founded in 1207, sheds light on why King John saw this as a suitable place for a new town. The area of England which was to become Merseyside was, in the twelfth century, a flat, poorly drained area, the lowlands consisting of bogs and mosses, with drier areas on the higher ground. The Moss Lake, once a feature of the area around Abercromby Square and Faulkner Square between Hope and Crown Streets, was typical of the landscape, and large areas of moss stretched to West Derby in the east and north, and Toxteth in the south. The River Mersey flowed to the west, with an inlet, the Pool, draining into the river from the north-east bank. The mouth of the Pool, into which the Moss Lake drained, was a body of sheltered, calm waters surrounding a short peninsula which formed the highest point in the area.

Inland were higher areas less eroded by the retreating glaciers which had carved out the lowlands and the Mersey itself. These hills were covered in heather and gorse, and spread from north-west to south-east, including Brownlow Hill in the town centre and the Everton Hills to the north-east.

PEOPLE AND VILLAGES

Since the time of the Norman Conquest in 1066 England had been governed under a feudal system. Under feudalism, the entire country belonged ultimately to the king, who gave property to those who provided loyal service. England was

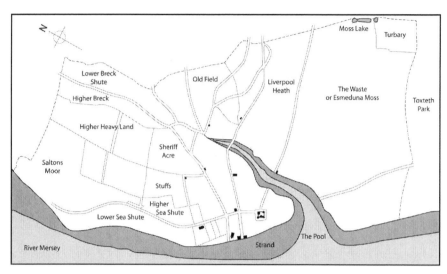

The landscape close to the new town of Liverpool was a heavy influence on the settlement's early history, and essential to the decision to found it in the first place. It had a sheltered harbour defended by a high promontory, on which the castle was built, and was surrounded by field systems, streams and mosslands which enabled or restricted the shape of development. (After Patmore, J.A. & Hodgkiss, A. G., *Merseyside in Maps*, p12, Fig. A, 1970, Longman)

divided into large areas known as hundreds, which were further divided into parishes, and lastly into manors.

West Derby was the largest hundred in Lancashire, and stretched from the Mersey to the River Ribble at Preston. Its administrative centre was in the village of West Derby, and whatever settlement existed at Liverpool at this time would have come under West Derby's jurisdiction.

As the Crown was the highest landowner, leasing land to his nobles, so those nobles in turn leased farms and manors to lower gentry. At the bottom of this pile were the common farmers. These people inhabited the villages and hamlets, sought protection in these dangerous times from the landlords, and in return farmed the land for themselves and their lords.

Domesday Book (1086) records several manors by name, including West Derby, Toxteth and Walton. Allerton may have been a small manor in its own right in the medieval period, centred on Allerton Hall. Surrounding the Hall would have been a series of minor estates, giving Allerton the feel of a collection of houses rather than a single community. Childwall, Belle Vale, Gatacre, Woolton, Fazakerley and Speke/Oglet would have been small farms within West Derby, and would have been the total settlement in the area. Doomsday does not name Liverpool itself, but does count six berewicks (literally 'wheat farms', outlying farms of the manorial seat) amongst the manor of West Derby. Liverpool is almost certain to have been one of these (along with Hale, Garston, Everton, Fazakerley and Great Crosby). These berewicks were near the bottom of the social hierarchy, and might have been little more than a handful of buildings. It may be that this handful of buildings was the form Liverpool took just before King John decided to intervene.

Windmills were an important part of the farming landscape. These were large buildings, and the key to feeding the population. As such, they belonged to the lord only, and commoners had to pay him in order to use the mill to grind their corn. This situation was common to the entire country, but would become of significant importance in the early centuries of Liverpool's history.

The manors and berewicks of West Derby hundred give clues in their place names to the nature of the landscape at the time of Liverpool's creation. Allerton contains place names including 'moss', such as Mossley Hill. The landscape here would have been marginal, and part of the waterlogged ground found all over Merseyside.

THE FOUNDATION OF LIVERPOOL

King John travelled from Lancaster to Chester in the early thirteenth century and crossed the Mersey at Warrington. It may have been on this trip that he first considered Liverpool as a place to develop as a borough. The location was attractive to John for many reasons.

The natural landscape could be exploited. The promontory around which the Pool flowed was a naturally defensible location, and the obvious place for a castle. The Pool itself was a safe harbour of calm waters. This could be used for both trading vessels and troop ships in times of war, even in stormy weather.

John's reign was characterised by wars with Ireland, amongst other places, and Liverpool was a perfect launching point for troops headed across the Irish Sea. It also had an advantage over Chester in that it was not controlled by a powerful earl. Once built, the town of Liverpool itself would also back up the troops, as it was able to supply them with accommodation, food, drink and other services such as boat and weapon repair.

The commercial potential of a new port town held many benefits for the king. Merchants making use of the port would own ships which could be taken and used to transport troops, and this occurred several times during Liverpool's early history. As the market town and borough were owned directly by the king (as part of his 'demesne'), dues and customs on goods would be paid directly to him, rather than via a bailiff of the local landlord. This meant that these duties could be lower, encouraging the further growth of the town. John's relationship with Liverpool continued to revolve around money, and it was later to be seen that, whenever the king needed extra cash, the town merchants would gladly pay John for even more rights (such as the collection of taxes and rents) than the initial charter had granted.

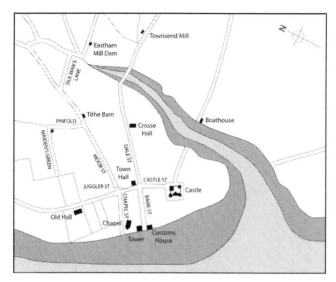

Taking a closer view, the appearance of the streets and burgages (commercial building plots) was typical of a newly established borough of this time. Suitable areas were established for markets, and the original street names reflect something historic about each road itself. (After Patmore, J.A. & Hodgkiss, A.G., *Merseyside in Maps*, p12 Fig. A, 1970, Longman)

The shape of the town

At Liverpool's inception seven streets were laid out, forming an H-shape which stood with its feet on the banks of the Mersey. The two streets which ran inland were Bank Street (now Water Street) and Chapel Street. Joining these together at their inland end was Juggler (now High) Street, with Dale Street and Tithebarn Street continuing further inland from these roads respectively. The White Cross, a stone monument with five stone steps, stood at the top of Chapel Street, with Whiteacre Street (now Old Hall Street) running north from here. At the junction of High Street and Water Street was the High Cross, with Castle Street (possibly a later addition) running south. The houses which were built along these roads had long gardens, or crofts, running behind them. Rent for these 'burgages' was one shilling a year, and by 1300 168 had been bought (more on this below).

The town itself was surrounded by fields. There was enclosed land to the north which was used for strip and arable farming. Each person who farmed the land would have been allotted two or three strips, with one set aside to produce food for the local landlord (whether the monarch or local lord). Everyone in the town would have contributed time in their year to work on this land, and the reeve, who worked for the bailiff of West Derby, would collect rents on behalf of the lord.

The Townfield lay to the north, along with the Oldfields, Dalefield and Heathy Lands. More fields lay to the east, which were also probably cultivated, although the land between the Pool and Toxteth Park was known as the Waste, and was not put into productive use until later. The stream which flowed from the Moss Lake down the hill into the Pool at the bottom of William Brown Street had a water-mill on it. This was the king's mill, and all the inhabitants of early Liverpool had to grind their corn there, and paid for the privilege.

The religious beliefs of the citizens of Liverpool were served from early on by the chapel of Mary del Key, which stood on the waterfront at the bottom of the aptly named Chapel Street. St Nicholas' church, which remained a chapel of ease for the parish of Walton-on-the-Hill until the seventeenth century, was built soon after as the town grew, and the smaller chapel was re-used as a school and a warehouse over its history.

Burgages and burgesses

A key part of the new settlement was the system of burgages which were laid out across the town. When King John granted the charter to Liverpool, the system which developed in order to promote growth was centred on attracting new burgesses to the town to take advantage of the reductions in dues and other tolls.

'Burgage' is the name given to the fixed plot of land which a merchant would use for business, and would include a building on the street from which he (or occasionally she) would do business. The burgess, the owner of the burgage, would also live in the building with their family, perhaps using the front-most rooms as offices or shop space.

The burgess himself would be a free man, meaning he was not subservient to a lord. Normally, a commoner was tied to the land, farmed it for the lord and was little more than the lord's property. If the commoner could make it to a free borough, and gain a place to live and work, they would automatically become free. A burgess of a town was also considered a 'local', and this conferred benefits over those who travelled from further afield to Liverpool markets (such as the weekly Saturday market and the November St Martin's Day Fair). Burgesses would not have to pay taxes on transactions, whereas their 'foreign' counterparts from Preston, Manchester, or Ireland would. At market, locals would pay a nominal fee to have a stall, whereas the local bailiff could demand any price to charge those from elsewhere.

So those entrepreneurial spirits who answered John's call to set up shop in the new borough would find themselves operating out of a home and shop in one, with preferential treatment when transacting business. There was an incentive to get a burgage early, as in theory there was a limited number of plots

The 'Sanctuary' stone in Castle Street is a reminder of one of the oldest activities in the town. It is the only one of four stones used to mark the limits of the markets held on St Martin's Day (11 November) and St James's Day (25 July). For the duration of the market, and for ten days either side, no court summons could be issued or arrests carried out. Instead justice was meted out immediately by officer of the Crown.

available and the benefits were significant. Liverpool also had a large hinterland, with Lancashire and Cheshire nearby, Staffordshire and the Midlands not far beyond, and easy sea links along the coast to Wales and Scotland, and across the sea to Ireland.

We can assume that there was a very low number of people in Liverpool before the town was founded. There may have been less than half a dozen families in 1207, but by the end of Liverpool's first century, poll tax returns show that there were around 800 people in 168 burgages. By the middle of the fourteenth century this had risen to around 1,000 people, although the population was soon to be decimated by the Black Death in 1349 and the bubonic plague in around 1360. At these times of crisis the parish church of Walton-on-the-Hill could not cope with the number needing burial, and a licence was obtained from the Bishop of Lichfield to allow the use of St Nicholas' churchyard as a burial ground.

Powerful families

Despite the relative freedom granted to any ordinary person who wanted to operate in the town, Liverpool was dominated by a small number of very influential families. Some of these were noble families, others were landed gentry and still more simply gained influence through successful commercial ventures once settled on the banks of the Mersey.

The Molyneux family were perhaps the most powerful in south-west Lancashire, having held the manor of Sefton since at least 1100. They were rewarded with lands by William the Conqueror in return for their support at the Battle of Hastings, and had an established power base in the West Derby area. Their power was exemplified by the tithe barn which they built in Tithebarn Street in the sixteenth century. This was where every family in the town paid their tithe, and so a profitable Liverpool meant a profitable Molyneux family. For much of its history Liverpool Castle was in the hands of the Molyneux, lending them a town centre base to compliment their lands at Sefton. They often came into conflict with the other powerful family of the time, the Stanleys.

The Stanley family were owners of the Tower, a fortified house on the waterfront at the bottom of Water Street. Having owned the house for several years already, they were authorised to embattle (fortify) it in 1406, thus adding a power base to balance that of the Molyneux in Liverpool Castle. The embattling of the house came at a time of a weak king, Henry IV, which allowed this relatively minor gentry family to strengthen its position to rival that of the greater power of the Earl of Sefton. The base of the Stanley family had recently expanded to include Lathom and Knowsley, and Thomas Stanley cemented his influence when Henry VII made him Earl of Derby.

The Moores were a family of burgesses, who owned a large house – Moore, or Old, Hall on Old Hall Street – as well as their burgage plots. Moore Hall was built in 1236, and this early investment in the town shows the family's confidence in the success of Liverpool. Similarly, the Crosses were a wealthy family who built

The Tower at the bottom of Water Street and the castle at the south end of Castle Street became the two great centres of fortified power in the town. The buildings were owned by the Stanleys and the Molyneux respectively, representing an uneasy standoff which occasionally erupted into skirmishes and violence between the two factions. (From Muir, R., *A History of Liverpool*, 1907, plate 3 & 4, Liverpool University Press)

Crosse Hall on Dale Street. Their property extended right back from Dale Street to the Pool, and their wealth increased upon them taking ownership of the fee farm (the right to collect dues in the town) in the 1470s.

There were several other families of importance in the formative years of Liverpool's history. The Norris family built Speke Hall several miles south of the town near the river; the de Ferrers held the title of the Earl of Lancaster, were naturally influential in West Derby and Liverpool, and built Liverpool Castle in the 1230s. As members of the established order, the de Ferrers occasionally came into conflict with the burgesses, who were gradually accumulating rights and powers previously unavailable at that level of society.

Increasing the control of the burgesses

As Liverpool expanded, so did its ambitions. The town grew beyond the size of rivals such as Preston and Chester, and at the same time the burgesses attempted to accumulate as much power as possible, at the expense of the wealthier nobles.

Fortunately for the town King Henry III found himself desperate for money in 1229 and, on 24 March that year, he agreed to sell a new charter to the merchants for £6 13s 4d. This gave them the power to elect their own officers, rather than be governed by a bailiff, and the ability to settle property cases in the 'Portmoot' court under their own jurisdiction. It freed them from attending the twice-yearly West Derby court which derived from that township's ancient hold on power, and freedom from paying royal tolls throughout the country. The charter also gave them the ability to form a guild to administer trade in the borough. The trade guild could prevent any non-member from trading in the town, or extend burgess-like rights to those who didn't own a burgage.

The very next day the burgesses also bought the fee farm (the right to collect rents) from Henry for £10. The royal bailiff could now be dispensed with altogether, and the merchants were now in charge of collecting burgage rents, fees and fines paid by travelling merchants, fees and fines from the Portmoot court, profits from the town's mills, and all profits from the running of the ferry, a service mentioned as long ago as Domesday. This accumulation of power meant effectively that Liverpool merchants were self-governing: they ran their own courts, they paid rent to themselves, and they ran their own mills and ferry.

In the coming years this power was not always left unchecked, and the Earls of Lancaster frequently attempted to take back some of the powers gained by these agreements. The rights to collect market tolls, profits from the mills and ferry, and later the fees and fines from the Portmoot, all had to be regained, having been lost to the earls in 1266.

At the start of the fourteenth century the burgesses leased the Salthouse Moor, north of Liverpool, from Thomas of Lancaster, who also granted them 12 acres of peat near the top of Brownlow Hill for 1*d* a year. In 1357 they were granted a lease of the whole town, by Henry, Earl of Lancaster, for 50 marks (£33 6*s* 8*d*) for ten years. This was a fantastic investment on the burgesses' part, as they now had control of the management of markets and fairs, ferries, mills, court fees and rent collection. To go with this around sixty years later all residents of Liverpool came under the jurisdiction of the borough courts. Before this point those people living on Salthouse Moor to the north of the town, or Brownlow Hill to the east, came within the authority of the Earl of Lancaster. Now a larger area was subject to the freedoms of the borough, away from the control of the lord. As part of these powers the burgesses nominated their own 'major ballivus' – chief bailiff, or mayor – and a nascent town council was born. The most influential burgesses formed themselves into a self-organised group, the aldermen, and the town was effectively controlled by its own merchants. In 1393, John of Gaunt granted the town practically all the dues, fine and lord's rights in the entire town, from the walls of the castle to the edge of Toxteth Park. This process of accumulating land and power was effectively the beginning of the existence of Liverpool Corporation, although this term was not used at the time.

TUDOR LIVERPOOL

The Tudor period saw little change in the town of Liverpool. While its burgesses continued to expand their control of the town and constantly grew in power and influence, when it came to national matters, and the affairs of state conducted in London, Liverpool remained an inconsequential backwater, isolated from the circles of power and on the wrong side of the country to benefit much from European ties.

However, it was a naturally independent borough, with its own market, a large hinterland and links with Ireland, Wales, Scotland and the Isle of Man. With little influence from London, it was in turn unaffected by events such as the Armada, Reformation or growing French trade. Its seven founding streets were still the core of the town, and although bustling with its chapel and school, every citizen would have known every other person in Liverpool.

By this time the castle had fallen into ruins, politics was a sport for the upper gentry to play with Liverpool as their game ball, and although the city had overtaken Chester in terms of the size of its port, it may have been that this wasn't realised by the Liverpolitans. It certainly wasn't capitalised on, and Liverpool remained small right through the Tudor period.

Tudor people

The population of Liverpool was a mixture of wealthy people and poor. The richer members of society lived on Water Street – the centre of town – while the rest lived towards the outskirts. In 1548 there were around 500-600 people and this slowly grew as the century wore on. By 1600 there would have been around 1,000 people living in Liverpool, despite a third of citizens being killed by an outbreak of the 'Sweating Sicknesse' in 1557.

The growth in population can be attributed to migration from Lancashire, Cheshire and the Wirral, but there was also a high turnover – few families could trace a presence in the town over more than a couple of generations.

Soldiers could also be garrisoned in the town. King John's intentions at the founding of Liverpool were dependent on the town being a base for soldiers, and right into the Tudor period Liverpool could be empty of troops and ships, or overrun with soldiers awaiting a favourable tide to take them to Ireland, Scotland or mainland Europe.

Education and society

Education of boys (never girls) was provided by a school operating in the chapel of Mary del Key and later St Nicholas' church. The school was set up using a donation in John Crosse's will of 1515, and as a result literacy slowly and steadily improved. Teachers were chosen by the mayor and aldermen and the salary was paid by the town. Later on the Duchy of Lancaster paid the majority of the salary, with some help from the town. Teachers had more often than not been educated at Farnworth School near Widnes.

It is known that a number of Liverpool's inhabitants attended university. This was not cheap – it cost between £20 and £50 a year to attend (around £7,500 in today's money), plus all the necessary clothes, furniture, sheets and other paraphernalia which were required by a full-time student. Consequently, only the sons of the more wealthy Liverpudlians went, most often to Brasenose College in Oxford.

Social mobility was restricted in Tudor England, even in an independent town such as Liverpool. A person's place in society was of great importance, especially in a small place where everyone likely knew everyone else. There were many pressing issues for people making their way in the world.

As population increased in the later Tudor period, efforts were made to deal with the problem of the poorer end of society. There were many discussions surrounding the 'deserving' poor. This problem was solved in towns such as Norwich, Ipswich and London by implementation of the Poor Laws. However, this did not occur until later in Liverpool, and this may have been because the number of poor people in the town was relatively low. The main concerns were that poor families would arrive in the town, and have children who would then be the legal responsibility of Liverpool to look after. Therefore poor incomers were discouraged from staying long. An alternative viewpoint is that in Liverpool everyone but the super-rich could be considered 'poor' – poor people did not stand out from the crowd. Although some specific cases of helping the poor are recorded, only sporadically were the Poor Laws enacted or fines given out.

Other issues with the 'lower' classes were dealt with – dice and other gambling games were banned, and public houses were encouraged to enforce this ban. However, only minor attempts were made to back up this suppression. The town was small enough to limit the amount of crime which went on, although reports of disorderliness by the 'wait' (town musician) led to him losing his job repeatedly, and lewd behaviour and other petty crimes are recorded. Soldiers billeted in the Tower or castle were another common source of complaint, and were considered the source of the worse cases of crime.

The wealthier citizens had more egotistical worries, such as how close they were allowed to sit to the mayor when attending St Nicholas' church. Liverpool was an independent town, with no one person in control. The mayor and aldermen, who were also the most active members of the commercial class, played the greatest role in politics, and the town proved itself able to self-organise when the need arose. When epidemics of illness arose, cabins were constructed out on the heath to the north-east, and sick people were made to live out there until they recovered. This practice likely saved a lot of lives, and shows how the town could mobilise itself to react to challenging circumstances.

On St Luke's Day each year (18 October) the burgesses assembled to elect a new mayor, with the more minor offices elected the following day. Often the landed gentry, important families, such as the Norrises, Stanleys and Molyneux, would be given honorary mayoral titles. The more active and influential burgesses, such as Giles Brook and John Bird, appear repeatedly on the role of influential aldermen. Liverpool elected its first MP in 1545, but the town's influence in Parliament was questionable. The interests of the powerful noble families were usually influential factors in the conduct of these MPs. It wasn't until the election of Ralph Sekerston in 1562 that Liverpool began to take a proper interest in London politics, and Sekerston remained an MP until his death in the 1570s. But despite this, for the thirty years following his passing, Liverpool nominated no further MPs to Westminster.

Tudor religious practice

Partly due to its isolation from changing fashions and the politics of London and other parts of the country, Liverpool remained a rather conservatively religious town well into the Tudor period. The Reformation and Henry VIII's closure of the monasteries had little effect, as the nearest religious house was Birkenhead Priory across the river. The priory had operated the ferry, but this business passed into Crown and then Liverpool citizen hands so the disruption in service would have been hardly visible. Although fines were used to enforce Protestant conformism, this is not recorded as happening often in Liverpool. The town was slow to adopt the new religion, but not an active agent in resisting the change. As time went on, however, clinging to the old religion became something of a social faux pas rather than anything more serious, and it was at this stage that Protestantism began to take hold. Liverpool was a faraway town to many people in England, and as long as peace was kept then there were few people to be much concerned with Liverpool's recusancy.

St Nicholas' church was well cared for by the town. It is recorded as being 'adorned' in Queen Mary I's reign, possibly as part of a genuine local resurgence in Catholicism following her accession. Alternatively, the still secretly Catholic town may have felt able to publicly reinstate the imagery hidden by whitewash during the Reformation. The church was also given a slate roof in the Tudor period, and a mason was hired to rebuild it after it suffered damage in storms in 1565.

Living in Tudor Liverpool

Well into the Tudor era Liverpool remained a town of seven streets. The wealthier still lived in the most expensive houses on Water Street, as well as Castle Street and Dale Street. It may be that the proximity of the castle and the anchorage of the Pool kept prices high in these streets. The smaller and cheaper houses were on Chapel Street, Moore Street, Milne Street and Juggler Street.

Houses were either single or two storey, two or three rooms, and built of wood and plaster. Wills show that most residences, even if living comfortably, were by no means wealthy. Modest collections of silver, pictures, hangings and furniture were typical. With low population pressure the only new houses to be built were those of the rich, who built their own homes. Housing very slowly spread down Tithebarn Street, and Pool Lane formed to the south of the castle.

Despite these modest dimensions, Liverpool was labelled a 'neat and populous' town by William Camden in 1586, and John Leland in his journal found it worthy of comment that the streets were paved, suggesting that it had been this way for around 200 years already. Even a mostly uncomplimentary report prepared for Queen Elizabeth in 1559, which described how the rain got into the castle through holes in the roof, and that repairs were needed to the walls, noted with some optimism that, should the repairs be undertaken, the castle would make a suitable place to hold the queen's wapentake court, which historically had been held in West Derby (for a period, in the 1586-built courthouse which still stands in the village).

The centre of life could be said to be the common hall, given to the town in John Crosse's will of 1515. The upstairs was used as a meeting room for the town

Although no buildings survive from this early period in Liverpool's history, architecture which has survived in nearby towns can give a flavour of what the homes and shops of the sixteenth century would have looked like. These buildings in Chester (left) and Gateacre (right) display some of the common architectural styles which would be seen in Liverpool at the time, although the Gateacre building is a Victorian construction.

guild, and also as a court room. Downstairs was used as a warehouse, customs house, and a prison for freemen and common criminals.

Industry in the sixteenth century

Tudor Liverpudlians earned their living through a variety of means. Almost all were farmers, and may even have been partly self-sufficient in food by the standards of the day. Farming was often combined with other activities, such as brewing, tanning, pottery production, coal extraction or textiles. Parts of Merseyside were covered with poorly drained moss land, and so the poorer the location was for agriculture, the more the people who inhabited it supplemented their income with small-scale industries. Milling was a seasonal activity and, although profitable and therefore jealously guarded, meant that millers switched to farming when not operating their mill. Mills were multiplying across the landscape as population grew. The Eastham and Townsend mills were present by the fifteenth century, and other mills were to be found in West Derby, Garston and Wavertree.

Regulations concerning the use of the town by farmers show that it was of concern to the people. Burleymen were appointed to monitor the use of the Town Field, and Hayward and Moss Reeves did a similar job on the heath to the east of the town. Peat cutters were allowed in Toxteth, and animals were eventually allowed to pasture in Toxteth Park. In 1604 the owner of the Park, the Earl of Derby, having successfully petitioned Elizabeth I to allow disparking, sold the land to the Molyneux family, who leased it out to farmers, and the agricultural development of Toxteth began in earnest.

The industrial efforts of Liverpool's inhabitants did lead to problems. Refuse piled up in the streets; butchers, tanners and weavers discharged the water from their works into public water sources and the Pool; and farmers, despite regulations, let animals wander around the town, often causing damage and chaos.

Most people engaged in an industry worked from home, as they had done since the original burgage plots were laid out in the thirteenth century. Goods produced were mostly sent to market in town, but could find their way much further afield, or turned into finished products in the town for later sale. Tanners were a good example of this, producing leather which was made into shoes, saddles, harnesses and other articles in Liverpool. Weavers were also a common feature, and were part of many different industries, such as cloth-making and the production of sails and ropes for ships. Blacksmiths and carpenters produced goods or provided services for the town, such as panelling the common hall or repairing boats in the Pool. Many inhabitants were mariners, fishing in the Mersey and seas near Liverpool, and benefiting from other marine industries. Finally, general labourers could be found in Tudor Liverpool. Many who came to the town from elsewhere to find work often ended up in this general category, and could take part in almost any industry or craft which required the manpower.

The market for Liverpool goods had both near and distant elements. Locally, Liverpool was in competition with Ormskirk, Prescot, Warrington, Frodsham, Wallasey and Chester. Goods from these places were often exported through Liverpool's port, especially as tolls were lower through Liverpool than they were through its next biggest rival, Chester. The local market in Liverpool attracted traders from Shrewsbury, Gloucester, Wales, Chester, Formby, Everton, Kirkdale, Crosby, Woolton, Huyton and Prescot. Coastal shipping saw trade take place with Wales, Scotland, Ireland and the Isle of Man. Trade with Europe was regular if not very large. French, Spanish and Portuguese ports were traded with, although the changing nature of foreign relations meant that

Liverpool was founded as a mercantile centre, if only to help add funds to the king's coffers. Its coastal position allowed it to establish trade links early on, and by the sixteenth century ships were leaving the Mersey heading for Mediterranean and Atlantic ports, and returning with goods from across Europe.

sometimes this trade was difficult to carry out, and foreign pirates were always a danger at sea.

The weekly Liverpool market was a place to buy butter and eggs beside the High Cross; grain in Castle and Dale Street (Lancashire merchants on the east side of the street, Cheshire men on the west). Livestock was meant to be sold in the area around the castle, though it proved difficult to keep them in check. Coal, meat, grain, fruit, vegetables, dairy, wool and local crafts were all on offer.

Even here native Liverpudlians had the upper hand, as non-locals could not buy until one hour after the market bell rang to commence trade. Preston and Chester were rivals in terms of size and influence, but Liverpool had a more attractive port. Manchester cloth was exported, and Yorkshire, Cumbria and Cheshire goods all passed through the town and port.

Liverpool did not rise far above its small roots before the end of the Tudor period. It remained a similar size to the town which King John founded, although trade both domestic and foreign was gradually increasing. In the seventeenth century Liverpool would be caught up in a national crisis – the English Civil War – and would begin to develop into the important town that became the second city of empire.

CHAPTER 3

CIVILWARANDTHESEVENTEENTH AND EIGHTEENTH CENTURIES

The beginning of the seventeenth century witnessed an event in which Liverpool was to play its first prominent role on the national stage. The Civil War erupted in 1642, at a time when Liverpool was probably content to keep itself to itself. The town had grown rich on the independence that it enjoyed, and was most happy when left to get on with its business. However, all this was to change as the town's geographical setting led it to become a strategic target for both sides in the conflict.

At the beginning of the war Liverpool was surrounded by land-holding Royalists and, as a conservative town, was itself on the side of the king. Despite trying to keep its distance from the conflict, both the Royalists and Parliamentarians realised early on that the port provided access to the Irish Sea, and as a result Liverpool remained an important outpost when the Civil War continued in Ireland into the 1650s. Furthermore, Manchester and the Mersey Valley beyond Liverpool were large areas of land held by Parliamentarians, and so Liverpool could be decisive in the balance of power in the north of England.

The town changed hands several times in the early years of the war, and Lord Strange (formerly the mayor and later Earl of Derby) seized the town magazine in 1642 for the Royalists. John More, the most important man in Liverpool at the time, withdrew from the town which was then garrisoned under the Royalist Captain, David Lloyd. This was a period of Royalist dominance, but they were defeated at Whalley in Lancashire in 1643, and the town was once again captured by the Parliamentarians in May of that year.

Nevertheless, the Royalists drew up plans to re-take Liverpool, and with it Lancashire. Prince Rupert was sent to take York and then Liverpool, and the town succumbed to siege and bombardment from the prince, who camped on Everton Hill, on 11 June 1644. The battle for Liverpool was hard fought, because the defences set up by the Parliamentarians – a great mud wall, strong town gates and cannon emplacements based around the castle – held well, assisted by ships in the harbour. Around 400 men were killed in the action, indicating just how valuable the town was.

Rupert intended to upgrade the defences to the designs of the renowned defence architect, Bernard de Gomme, but this was never carried out. Perhaps for this reason the Parliamentarians again took Liverpool before the end of the year, and John More returned as governor.

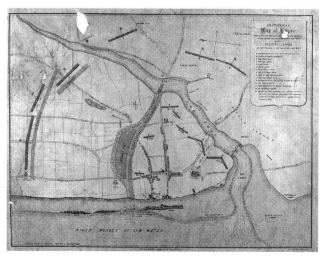

Despite its attempts to keep clear of the conflict, Liverpool became a strategic target during the Civil War. Earthern banks were erected around the town boundary, and gates were erected on Dale Street to control entry. These were pulled down soon after the war, although proposals were made for more substantial defences which were never completed. (Liverpool Record Office, Liverpool Libraries)

LIVERPOOL'S SELF-GOVERNANCE

The Civil War had been a blow to Liverpool's ambitions as an independent mercantile town, tossed as it was on the winds of change. However, in the years which followed, the town's civic elites began a process of gaining back the independence they had lost, finally removing the influence of the landed nobility on the town forever.

In 1626 Charles I had granted another charter, part of a series given to Liverpool in its 400-year history. This new charter confirmed the borough and its powers, including the full control of legislation by the burgesses, confirmed the right to hold a court under the Statute of Merchants, and stated that the town held control over the Waste. This would make available land to build on and develop when Liverpool later began to get overcrowded.

However, the noble families were still vying for control with the merchants and citizens of Liverpool. Lord Strange, the mayor, still claimed a veto over elections. In 1632 the first Viscount Molyneux, Earl of Sefton, bought the Crown rights of Liverpool effectively becoming lord of the manor. This was in contradiction to the freedom from lordly influence granted by previous charters, and gave Molyneux the rights over the common, the Waste, the waters and other tolls of the town in perpetuity. Because a good sign of the town's independence was the right to collect its own tolls and rents, this represented a blow to the power of the aldermen. Both the earls of Sefton and Derby became mayor in their time, and the families remained powerfully influential in Liverpool no doubt to the chagrin of the merchants.

In the 1580s Liverpool had started sending two MPs to London, one of whom was nominated by the town (the council) and the other by the king (the king being, in effect, the local landowner). The first pair were Arthur Atye and John Molyneux, and townsmen were returned to Parliament until 1661. For ten years after this none were sent, however, and this allowed the Crown to increase its control over Liverpool. Following the Restoration of the Monarchy, Liverpool found it increasingly difficult to avoid the influence of the king, compared to the relative freedom enjoyed under the influence of the Stanleys, and other local families, previously. In fact the town seemed willing to submit partly to the influence of the Stanleys in return for their protection. It may have been considered more useful to counter the king's influence in this way, at least for a while.

Other events show the town in conflict with its local landowners. Caryll Molyneux, a generally unpopular character at the time, attempted in 1668 to lay out a new road across the Pool from the orchard adjacent to his castle. The merchants decided that this was against their interests, and resolved to remove any bridge which was constructed. The bridge was begun in any case, but was demolished on the orders of the council in 1671. This action led to a compromise between the two factions: Molyneux built his road, Church Street, as intended, but sold to the town all his rights and privileges for £30 for 1,000 years. The only exception to the rights sold were the ferry tolls and burgage rents on his land, which normally were paid to the town anyway.

The process of gaining practical independence from lordly influence gained speed when, over the course of a few years in the seventeenth century, the town leased from their respective owners both the castle and the Tower. Over time the rights to demolish these powerfully symbolic buildings was bought by the aldermen, leading to the disappearance of these landmarks from the Liverpool landscape. With them went the power bases of the two most powerful families in the region.

The next stage in the evolution of Liverpool self-control was the issue of the parish church. The church of St Nicholas on the waterfront was a chapel of ease within the parish of Walton-on-the-Hill. This meant that religious matters were controlled from outside the town, and the inhabitants of Liverpool itself had to be buried in the churchyard at Walton. The latter problem became an important issue during outbreaks of plague which haunted the towns from the thirteenth to fifteenth centuries, but it was the former issue, that of spiritual control, that Liverpool, as an ever-expanding and proud town, felt it should have.

Matters came to a head in the closing years of the seventeenth century, when Liverpool refused to pay for repairs to Walton's church. This was simply money that was leaving the town, and which the council would prefer to see spent closer to home. The dispute led to renewed calls for Liverpool to be made its own parish. Parliament was petitioned, and in 1699 Liverpool was granted parish status. St George's church, Liverpool's first parish church, was constructed on the site of the demolished castle. From the eighteenth century Liverpool's councillors would ostentatiously parade from the Town Hall, down Castle Street to St George's each Sunday. This was a very visual demonstration and exhibition of the power brokers of Liverpool, and the symbolism of new power worshipping on the remains of the old would likely not have been lost on the participants.

Liverpool was a burgeoning town. The power and wealth generated by the merchants, traders and mariners, and embodied in the exploding population flowing into the town, was in the hands of local men. They had demanded, leased and bought almost all the rights traditionally held by the monarch or local lord. The town was poised to fully enter the Industrial Revolution with an active, entrepreneurial elite. Trade and politics went hand in hand, with one operating to the benefit of the other. At the same time, Chester, the rival and indeed more successful port for so long, was suffering a decline. This was partly due to the silting up of the Dee, but also the rise of a Mersey port which could control, and so lower, the dues paid by incoming ships. Liverpool was its own master at the end of the seventeenth century.

BECOMING AN EARLY MODERN TOWN

Tudor citizens of Liverpool had lived in an essentially medieval town, and the seven streets laid down in 1207 were still the main thoroughfares at the beginning of the seventeenth century. The technology simply did not exist to alter the landscape or improve the waterfront to any extent. The architecture of the town was vernacular: timber-framed buildings with walls of wattle and daub filled with rubble and stone. Roofs were thatched, and first and even second storeys jutted out above the lower ones. Although Liverpool was blessed with paved streets, as Daniel Defoe and others thought worthy of pointing out in their travel journals, the highways out of town were at best dirt tracks and at worst impassable quagmires.

But society was changing, and the physical character of the town of Liverpool began to change along with it, reflecting the social mores of the day. Where once houses had had few rooms – perhaps two or three – increasingly more divisions and rooms were added, improving privacy in the home. People were becom-

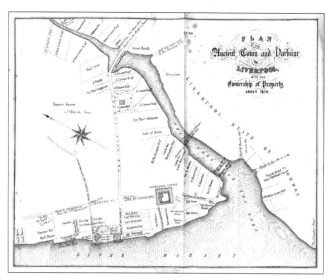

By the seventeenth century much of the town centre had assumed a familiar form. Although still small, Liverpool was starting to expand, with a bridge over the Pool built by Lord Molyneux. The castle was replaced with St George's church, consecrated by 1734. (After 'Plan of the Ancient Town and Harbour of Liverpool' in Baines, T., *History of Liverpool*, 1852)

ing more private, and the division between public spaces and private areas was becoming written into the very fabric of their houses.

Along with changes in interior spaces, the building materials were shifting with fashions and the availability of greater wealth to express an interest in it. Building materials like brick, stone and ashlar made their way into new houses. The richer merchants were the first to take advantage of these materials, but this drove a demand for them lower down the social (wealth) scale. Any fashion which first surfaced in London soon spread to Liverpool, which emulated its larger cousin in more than one way as the seventeenth and eighteenth centuries progressed, and gradually more and more house builders were able to afford these new technologies and styles.

The new materials were part of an increase in social display. To have a house built in the latest style, using the most fashionable materials, showed not only that you were successful and wealthy, but that you were up to date with the times. This led to a regular rebuilding of houses. Façades were repeatedly pulled down and rebuilt to keep up with trends. Interior spaces were redecorated, redivided and rebuilt accordingly.

As fashion became more important, and wealth increased amongst the merchant classes, even the objects you chose to decorate your home with could be used to demonstrate your standing in society. Homes were becoming more comfortable and elaborate, with hangings, fireplaces, chimneys, curtains and window glass all becoming part of maintaining your place on the modern social ladder.

THE TOWN IN THE SEVENTEENTH CENTURY

In 1600 Liverpool was still a very compact town. The Exchange, the centre of mercantile affairs where most of the town's trading took place, still lay at the heart of the town. Many merchants lived within walking distance, such as on Dale Street and Water Street. From here they could hear of news at the Exchange as soon as possible, and watch the flags on Bidston Hill on the Wirral which would tell them when one of their ships was coming in to port.

However, in the later seventeenth century Liverpool began to expand at a rate not seen before in its history. This expansion was haphazard, and led to overcrowding. Duke Street was one of the first roads to be laid out as part of Liverpool's early expansion. Merchants moved here and built their houses, warehouses and offices. Merchants who had decided to retire from business most often moved to the St Domingo estate in Everton, as well as other outskirts. From here they could enjoy their wealth in their later years, away from the noise and pollution of the town. More Street and Fenwick Street were built in 1670, and Old Hall Street and Lord Street were begun a few years later. In 1677 ten new streets, including James Street, Lancelot's Hey and Hackin's Hey, were laid out.

Mount Pleasant, Duke Street and Rodney Street made up some of the first areas to be expanded into in the seventeenth century, as places for the increasing

As Liverpool began to expand and experience increased commercial success, it looked to other fashionable towns such as London, Norwich, Bristol and Bath, and sought to emulate them architecturally. These buildings in North John Street show the Classical style which became popular at this time. Although these buildings are from the early nineteenth century, they demonstrate building projects which paralleled fashions in other towns.

influx of merchants and citizens. Looking at these roads today, the care taken in the design and layout of this area is clear. The roads are wide, straight and regular. In contrast to the competitiveness between members of high society at the beginning of this era, it was becoming desirable to occupy a house very similar to your neighbours. In a way this showed your inclusion in society, part of the corporate town, by sharing your house façade with your peers. This was a change from the earlier period when privacy and individuality were on the rise. It demonstrated an increase in outward shows of solidarity and unity, and helped build people's feelings of belonging and civic pride. It was also the first time that the more socially mobile elements of society voted with their feet to escape the town to the more airy and refined hills on the edge of Liverpool.

The transformation of the town was accelerated by increased contact with other towns. With improvements in roads into the hinterland, mail and passenger coaches gradually improved their service. The first stagecoach arrived from London in 1761 and within five years there were two coaches to London (taking as little as two days in summer) and another to Manchester. Coach houses were located at convenient points in the town, such as inns in Castle Street, Water Street and Dale Street. Services were advertised with regular departures several times a week, and the coaches called at convenient way points along the journey, such as at Warrington on the way to Manchester, or Lancaster on the way to Kendal.

EFFORTS TO IMPROVE THE TOWN

As Liverpool grew in size and ambition, and contact with similar towns increased, efforts were made to develop the town in such a way as to present the best face to its visitors, as well as to become the type of town merchants of the stature of

Liverpolitans deserved. Just as polite society constantly improved its houses to keep up with national fashions, so civic Liverpool kept its own house in order.

Liverpool had outgrown its Town Hall, and so another, larger edifice was commissioned. John Wood of Bath was brought in to design the structure. Wood was fresh from great successes in his home town, with the Circus and Royal Crescent cementing his name amongst the wealthy classes. The foundation stone was laid at the junction of Dale Street and Water Street in 1748, and the celebrations at its opening lasted a week.

Wider issues faced a town which wished to impress in its grandeur. Roads were often full of potholes where residents had taken earth and stone for their own requirements. They were filled with refuse and sewage dumped in the roadway. In some parts of the town centre the lanes were webs of dingy, narrow and winding thoroughfares, a situation not becoming of somewhere aspiring to imitate the fashionable towns of Bath, London, Ipswich and the like.

Therefore, between 1771 and 1832 over £600 (£30,000 in today's money) was spent on road improvement schemes. The main project was to widen Castle Street to deal with the enormous amount of traffic it had to deal with. The Liverpool Improvement Act of 1786 included plans to expand the road so that the new Town Hall, when viewed from Derby Square, would sit in the centre. However, the extent of this scheme was scaled back, and today the Town Hall sits slightly to one side. Some widening did occur, and so the flagship road for Liverpool's commercial centre was established.

As well as constructing fashionable offices and houses, the civic minds of Liverpool sought to create a modern and attractive streetscape. Castle Street was until this time a relatively narrow thoroughfare for such a central location, and so in 1786 permission was given for an Improvement Act, part of which resulted in the demolition of one side of the street to reveal more of John Wood's fine Town Hall. ('The Town Hall of Liverpool of 1786', lithographed by Greenwood, H., after Herdman, W.G., from *Pictorial Relics of Ancient Liverpool*, 1843, plate 21)

Not only were the fashions of building style and road schemes emulating other towns, new roads in Liverpool simply named after their London counterparts, thus giving us Islington, Whitechapel, Paddington and Drury Lane.

The New Town of Edinburgh, considered a triumph of eighteenth-century town planning, was worth imitating, and in 1771 a Liverpool-born builder, Cuthbert Bisbrown, proposed 'New Liverpool' on land formerly owned by the Earl of Sefton just to the south of the existing settlement. Unfortunately this is one project which did not meet with success, and Bisbrown was bankrupt by 1776. The road name Upper Harrington Street, named after Isabella, the daughter of the second Earl of Harrington, is the only surviving evidence of this ambitious scheme.

Nature in the city

The measures taken to create a more genteel living space for the wealthy classes were based to some extent on a renewed love of, and respect for, nature. Nature had once been an unstoppable force: the boats bobbing on the river and the coastal buildings like the castle and Tower were at the mercy of the elements, and little could be done to alter the natural features on which the town sat. But this balance of power was changing somewhat. Nature was becoming a thing to overcome, to tame and control. Vast swathes of country seats were being moulded by Lancelot 'Capability' Brown at Chatsworth and Longleat, but even the smaller urban developments were of a similar theme. Nature had been tamed in the development of former farmland into smart avenues and public squares. Views across countryside were appreciated, but admired from a distance, with tooth and claw kept comfortably at bay. Tiny enclaves of nature were let in to the town in the form of spaces like Abercromby Square and Faulkner Square, safely contained, controlled and sanitized for polite consumption within a orderly rectangle of impressive merchants' houses on the edge of eighteenth-century Liverpool.

There was also a social element. Those who could afford to live in these 'out-of-town' locations did so to get away from their 'inferiors'. Those members of the town's elite (such as the aldermen and the mayor) not only wanted to demonstrate their independence from the traditional seats of noble power, but also the comfortable distance they occupied from the lower orders.

Once these well-planned and carefully executed streets were built, further measures were taken to keep them genteel. Regulations were drawn up to prevent the setting up of businesses in these exclusive residential areas. Further legislation prevented the operation of noisy and dirty steam engines nearby. Finally, cellar dwellings were outlawed, to make Liverpool a very pleasant town to live in. It is hard to know to what extent the ban on cellar dwellings was enforced, but until the huge pressures on living space created by later immigration this would not have been a problem.

SOCIETY AND POPULATION EXPANSION

As the seventeenth century began, Liverpool was just starting to gain importance and influence on a wider scale. The number of incomers was increasing and changing, from the predominantly merchant make-up of its early years to a greater mixture of traders, farmers and others trying their luck in the burgeoning town. It was the pressure on housing created by this influx of new people which led to the first major phase of expansion and building that Liverpool had experienced since its foundation. In addition, the very richest merchants were demonstrating an urge to move out of the town centre, and newer houses were built on farmland on all sides, in Everton, Toxteth and Edge Hill, to take advantage of the greater spaces enabled by these greenfield developments.

The biggest contributors to the population increase were Welsh and Irish immigrants, coming to seek their fortunes or take advantage of the rapid growth of the town. This process only increased as Liverpool's importance grew ever more quickly.

In 1664 the population was still only 1,300, but by the end of the century this had grown to 5,000, and 20 per cent of this larger population were mariners. In only another fifty years this had tripled to 15,000, but this growth was dwarfed by that of the next fifty years – in 1800 Liverpool had exploded into a town of 80,000 souls. For most of this period, population had doubled in every genera-

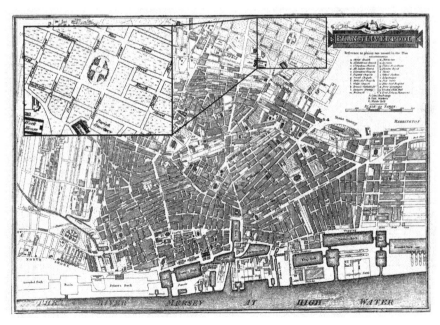

While the centre of town was being rebuilt, the richest merchants were moving to the first suburbs. Mosslake Fields was developed on the edge of town with fine views down to the Mersey. The predominant building fashions of the day were followed, creating long straight and uniform roads with Classical houses surrounding peaceful private gardens at Abercromby Square and Faulkner Square. (Gregory's *Plan of Liverpool*, 1825)

tion, starting out as a town smaller than Wigan (with 2,300 people) to overtake the great towns of the day such as Norwich (38,000), York (24,000) and Bristol (66,000). The population increase eventually began to take its toll, and by 1800 crowds of poor families were packed into slum houses and cellar dwellings, often with four people to a single room. The gap between the richest in society and the poorest was growing.

LEISURE TIME

Liverpool was a port city of great variety. The rich mingled with the poor and the permanent residents mixed with the sailors who attempted to make the most of their limited time ashore. The wealthiest classes, with their sanitised approach to appreciating 'nature', enjoyed a variety of outdoor pursuits, such as strolls through the elegant suburbs of Kirkdale and Toxteth, as well as cricket, horse-racing and cock-fighting. There was a bowling green on Mount Pleasant, a gravel walk on St James' Mount (adapted from a quarry in 1779), and Ladies Walk just to the north of the town centre was a pleasant path with views down to the Mersey. Ranelagh Gardens, on the site now occupied by the Adelphi Hotel, was the first public green space in Merseyside. It charged an admission fee and had a strict code of conduct. As such it was a place of genteel refuge on the edge of the still-growing town. The park held open-air concerts until 1796. In addition to Ranelagh Gardens, the Botanic Garden provided further outdoor entertainment when it opened in 1802.

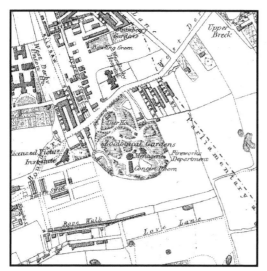 

A growing desire for genteel parks and walks led to the establishment of the first 'public' parks. These in fact were only accessible to the wealthier inhabitants of Liverpool, but provided fresh air and, in the case of the Zoological and Botanical Gardens, education and entertainment. (Extract from Davies' *Plan of Liverpool, Supplement to the Weekly Dispatch of Sunday December 16th, 1860*)

Festivals, fairs and markets were all social occasions, but were also chances to network, and exchange gossip about trade and industry. Any location or event could become a chance for informal gatherings, where socialising and business meetings could take place. The castle was one such place while it stood, used for plays before the Playhouse opened in Drury Lane. The Playhouse may have been a cockpit before it was turned into a theatre (with frankly little modification), and such sporting venues easily doubled as arenas for socialising with one's peers. The marketplaces also provided a venue where people would regularly gather.

The merchants also enjoyed socialising indoors. Coffee shops, inns and clubs provided a space where they could exchange news and views, get to know their friends and competitors, and escape the hurly burly of the Exchange floor. Exclusive indoor clubs opened their doors around the turn of the nineteenth century: the Anthenaeum in 1799, the Liverpool Library in 1758 (the first subscription library in England), the Royal Liverpool Institution in 1814 and the Lyceum in 1802.

RELIGIOUS DIVISIONS AND RELIGIOUS TOLERANCE

The Tudor period had seen the greatest change to religious practice in England's history. Henry VIII had broken away from the Church in Rome, and although England initially remained Catholic, Henry was now head of the Church in England. Later Tudor generations took England from Roman Catholicism to Protestantism and back again, and the Civil War period had also been one of religious conflict. The conservative members of society (which traditionally included the landowning elites) were more likely to remain Catholic, while more progressive town citizens were quicker to move to the new beliefs and practices of the Church of England. The relative influence of different factions had an effect on the dominant rituals in Liverpool, but in general it was a tolerant town by the standards of the day. If it had got in the way of trade it would have been a different matter, but as long as merchants could go to work, and ships to sea, then there was little to trouble Liverpool's civic leaders or inhabitants.

Around the time of the Civil War itself, there were hardly any Catholics in Liverpool. Even though the Crosse and Molyneux families were prominent members of this religion, and were occasionally singled out by agents of the church or government, the vast majority of Liverpool's citizens were Protestant, despite the fact that in many other ways the town was conservative. However, Liverpool was never dominated by Protestant churches. There were fourteen Anglican churches compared to thirteen 'dissenting' churches in 1800.

The toleration the town enjoyed in regards to religious belief may be seen in the sale of land in Toxteth Park by Lord Molyneux to a group of Puritans who wished to build a chapel. It remained an isolated enclave away from the town, which might explain why Molyneux was willing to sell, but it persisted, and marked the start of more intensive inhabitation of Toxteth compared to previous centuries. The Toleration Act of 1689 ensured that a variety of belief systems survived right across England, and this was nowhere more true than in the melting pot of Liverpool.

TRADE AND INDUSTRY LOCALLY

Liverpool was founded on the banks of the Mersey because King John saw its potential as a port. This was predominantly with the transport of troops to Ireland in mind, but the town itself was intended as a place to attract traders and merchants. Long before the town took advantage of its seaboard location, Liverpool was already benefiting from its large hinterland.

Salt was transported from Cheshire and exported from Liverpool. Coal from the west Lancashire coal fields came down the Mersey via St Helens, and both the coal itself and the products of St Helens' glass industry (itself made possible by the coal trade) found their way into the local economy.

Liverpool had long been the destination for farmers and other traders to come to market. A number of different markets had long existed around St George's church and its forerunner the castle, as well as on Dale Street and Castle Street. As the town became wealthier and more independent, market tolls decreased, thus boosting Liverpool's attraction for traders from Lancashire, Cheshire, Wales and the Midlands, and also further afield.

Despite the concentration on trade activities by the Liverpolitans of the time (as well as historians later) it must not be forgotten that there were a great many people in Liverpool who had other livelihoods. Clock-making was common around the end of the eighteenth century. The famous Herculaneum Pottery factory opened in Toxteth in 1794. Another famous cottage industry was the Everton Toffee Shop, which opened for business in 1753. In addition to the cloth trade, there were several practitioners of the silk trade, operating from (appropriately) Silkhouse Lane.

The Herculaneum Pottery was established in 1793 on the banks of the Mersey by Richard Abbey. It grew into a large factory which dominated the southern shoreline, and gave its name to the dock which was later built on the site. (Trustees of National Museums Liverpool)

The Corporation

As the merchant class developed, cooperation between them formalised, and Liverpool found itself with credit networks stretching as far as London. Partnerships developed, until eventually the Corporation emerged from the confluence of trade and politics. Whereas other important towns developed trade guilds which had control over different industries, Liverpool never had such guilds or other commercial societies.

The Corporation was effectively brought into existence when Thomas of Lancaster had leased land out to the merchants on Salthouse Moor at the start of the seventeenth century. This had extended the freedoms of the town further out than they had been before – beyond the town itself for the first time. The Corporation became not only the main political force in Liverpool (a charter of 1695 established a forty-strong council from the merchant classes, plus the mayor), but also slowly gained influence over the MPs the town returned to Parliament.

In 1660, for example, they refused to elect Sir Edward More (the main landholder at the time) as MP. They also refuted the claims on the common land made by Lord Molyneux. They won their case, and then received rents when the land was enclosed. Rental income for the Corporation increased from £300 to £1,200 between 1662 and 1700, cementing their power even further.

For centuries the Exchange Building had been the centre of mercantile activity. Liverpool had gone through at least two Exchanges, and by the middle of the eighteenth century the current Exchange was in need of expansion. The construction of the John Wood Town Hall was a landmark moment in Liverpool's ascendancy, and brought together the functions of Town Hall, Exchange and Assembly Rooms. Although a fire gutted the interior at the start of 1795 the main portion of the building was kept, with some redesigning and rebuilding taking place. The dome, to a design by James Wyatt, was added at that time.

TRADE OVERSEAS

Of course, the biggest source of wealth in Liverpool at this time was the burgeoning sea trade. In previous centuries Liverpool had seen its contacts grow with Scotland, Ireland, Wales and other coastal towns in southern England, but it also enjoyed a flourishing trade with the Continent – France, Portugal and Spain. However, these routes were risky in those years, with wars making any route through the channel dangerous, and contact with the enemy unthinkable.

Liverpool continued to trade in French and Spanish wine, for instance, in the following centuries. After the discovery of the New World, however, England and Liverpool in particular had a new market to exploit. Trade with Barbados consisted mostly of tobacco at first. Much of this managed to avoid customs dues as it was damaged in transit, though whether this damage restricted the profits of those who sold it is open to question. West Indian sugar found its way to the port, as well as foreign wool and cloth to compete with local products. Two voyages in

1666 brought back sugar, and the first sugar refinery was already in existence by 1667. This began Liverpool's long relationship with the sugar trade. Liverpool's trade destinations continued to diversify across the seventeenth century, the most varied and notorious of which were involved in the trade of enslaved Africans in the Americas (see below).

Trade with America and Ireland not only boosted Liverpool's economy, it also provided safer routes to trade, avoiding Dutch and French ships. Liverpool had this advantage over other English ports such as Dover and Southampton whose trade remained along the dangerous English Channel.

Exports were as important as imports. Local coal and salt from Lancashire and Cheshire left England via Liverpool, having travelled down the Mersey from their point of origin. A salt refinery built at Dungeon Rock, Hale, boosted the port, and a salthouse in Mersey Street supplied both the export trade and in-town glasshouses. These were examples of two local trades benefiting from both being situated in Liverpool. In the same way, coal from the St Helens coalfield could be processed with other local materials by Merseyside industry.

The fortunate proximity to these two key raw materials was essential to Liverpool's prosperity by the eighteenth century, to the extent that historian Jane Longmore has labelled them the 'twin pillars' of the town's success. Other factors also promoted the wealth of the town. Road links with Manchester and Staffordshire – two key areas for raw materials and manufactured goods – improved in the seventeenth and eighteenth centuries. Manchester linen was gaining a reputation for excellence, and Liverpool certainly benefited from being the place to acquire it.

Liverpool was becoming an increasingly accessible port, overtaking the less convenient Chester as the gateway to overseas markets. Chester's hinterland lacked the industrial activities that Liverpool's had, and even the slightly greater mileage between Chester and Dublin meant that Liverpool became the favoured port. In 1699 Liverpool had achieved another ambition: it gained its own customs house, and was finally freed from Chester. Administratively, Chester was the head port for a stretch of coastline from Lancaster to Anglesey and so customs and tolls were recorded there. Liverpool was classed as a 'creek' or 'haven' of Chester until the transfer of responsibility to the rising city.

Finally, Liverpool's relatively long history and experience as a town of merchants stood it in good stead. The naturally entrepreneurial spirit which inhabited both the citizens and, as has been mentioned, the council, meant that opportunities for expansion and the skill in trade was second to none. Although at the beginning of this period trade was still largely on an individual basis, as the Corporation gained power (and merchants essentially ran the town) it laid the foundations for Liverpool's later successes. Some mariners even became merchants at some point in their career, and so those who used Liverpool as their port may well have had an education in the trade at a grassroots level. Apprenticeships were available for those who looked to become merchants, whether former sailors or not. Liverpool thus became a town inseparable from its form and function as a port. Eyes' map of 1765 shows a whole host of buildings which were maritime in nature, from the docks and customs house to the roperies and shipwrights' yards.

Other trades essential to the operation of a port also grew. Around 27 per cent of the population were occupied with port industries such as carpentry and shipbuilding, and sailors were increasing as a proportion of the local inhabitants. Agriculture at this time had shrunk to only 1 per cent of local industry, revealing how it had been pushed out once Liverpool found its feet as a port.

DOCKS AND DOCKLANDS

Liverpool had a natural harbour in the form of the Pool. This inlet of the Mersey enjoyed calm waters and was protection from storms and enemy activity on the river. However, the town's trade quickly outgrew the Pool's docking facilities. Until the seventeenth century boats would simply tie up at the pier or jetty in the Pool, or cargo would be rowed ashore in smaller boats while the main ship stood anchored further out. The smallest cargo-carrying ships, if flat-bottomed, could rest on the mud flats when the tide went out. Their load could even be carried ashore by men, and the boat would return to sea on the next high tide.

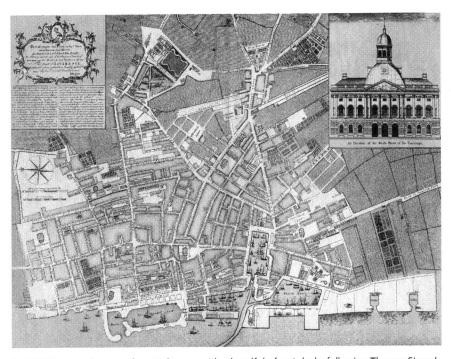

By 1765 Liverpool was a substantial town, with a handful of wet docks following Thomas Steers' pioneering Old Dock of 1715. On Eyes' map of 1726, the Pool is no longer a feature of the town, and roads built out towards Toxteth Park are taking the town south along Park Lane. (Liverpool Record Office, Liverpool Libraries)

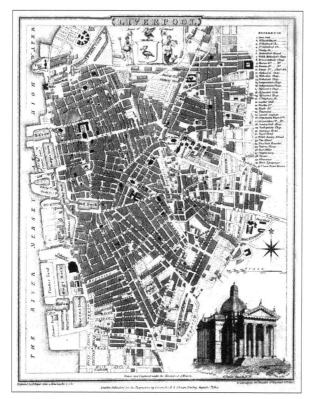

Once Liverpool had developed from a fishing and trading harbour into an impressive eighteenth-century town, much of the original natural landscape had disappeared. The Pool was now the Old Dock, and land was being reclaimed from the Mersey to build further basins. This ability – and willingness – to alter nature for commercial ends characterised the ambition and intentions of Liverpool's civic leaders right through history. This 1807 map shows what the town looked like at the end of the eighteenth century and the start of the nineteenth. (Cole & Roper's *Plan of Liverpool*, 1807)

But once trade took off, and boats became larger, the Pool started to become more of a hindrance than a help to Liverpool's trade. A quayside was ordered to be built below the castle in 1636, and a sluice gate was constructed which could release water to scour silt from the base of the Pool. The creek was at constant risk of silting up, partly from ships dropping ballast directly into its waters while docked.

Even this scheme could not ensure the continued growth of Liverpool trade, however. A solution was eventually engineered by Thomas Steers (a Kent-born man, later mayor of Liverpool). Steers designed and built the world's first commercial wet dock, eventually known as the Old Dock, in the mouth of the Pool. Construction began in 1709 and was completed in 1715, and at its opening it held 100 ships. It was a risky venture, with the whole of the Corporate estate mortgaged to pay for it, alongside loans and Acts of Parliament needed to fund the project, but it represented perhaps the greatest coming together of Liverpool's entrepreneurial, mercantile, engineering and civic prowess. The fact that Liverpool's roads still converge on the site of the Old Dock says something about the centrality of the shipping age to Liverpool's very fabric.

A wet dock is an enclosed dock with gates, allowing ships to enter at high tide, remain afloat when the tide goes out, and then return to sea via the gates once the external tide matches the water level within. For Liverpool, this meant that ships with deep berths could now unload directly onto the quayside, saving both time and money, reducing risk of damage, and making the town an even more attractive prospect to merchants.

Although trade suffered during the American Revolution and the tobacco trade collapsed in the 1720s and '30s, Liverpool had cemented its reputation as one of the most important ports in the country by the middle of the eighteenth century. Even by the start of the century Steers' Old Dock was proving to be inadequate for the growth of trade. Where, at first, the Old Dock had been accessible directly from the River Mersey, eventually ships entered via the Salthouse Dock, which was added to the dock estate in 1753. Salthouse was also designed by Steers, but was finished after his death by Henry Berry, Liverpool's second dock engineer.

This initiated a great programme of dock expansion by the Corporation, who were willing to invest vast sums into the venture. Over £4 million was spent in the 150 years from 1700 (over a quarter of a billion pounds in modern money). There was a thirty-fold rise in tonnage dealt with by Liverpool docks over the course of the seventeenth century, compared to a mere quadrupling of tonnage in Bristol, Liverpool's main rival. The Old Dock dealt with the Indian and African trades, plus shipping from Europe and Ireland, with the Salthouse Dock dealing with West Indian ships. Kings and Queens Docks, both opened in 1785, dealt with other American trades, the Kings also dealing with Baltic trade and the Queens with Greenland fishery ships.

THE ATLANTIC SLAVE TRADE

The trading of enslaved Africans was in existence before Liverpool became a major port. The Royal African Company had a legally enforced monopoly in the early eighteenth century, but the African Trade Act of 1750 lifted this monopoly, allowing others to enter the market. At the same time, American colonies were growing in size, and more labour was required to work them. Liverpool took advantage of the demand, coupling the slaving routes to its existing network of American ties. In addition, other Liverpool trades grew close links with that of the Atlantic slave trade and the colonies, such as sailors, iron merchants, drapers, gunsmiths, grocers, shipyard owners and property agents. As Liverpool grew around its shipping trades, so it grew around the passage of slaves from Africa to America, and today road names, memorials and friezes on several buildings in the city centre attest to the central role the trade played in the creation of wealth in the city.

What perhaps made possible the involvement of so many people in the slave trade, and possibly the later reversal of attitudes of prominent members of the Liverpool civic elite, was the distance – geographical and psychological – between the businessmen and the enslaved Africans. The Africans themselves were transferred on the so-called Middle Passage, between the Gold Coast and surrounding areas to the West Indies. The ship owners, based in Liverpool, remained removed from the horrors of this Middle Passage. The captains of the ships could distance themselves too – after all, they were 'only carrying out orders'. This was not always the case, though, and it is not surprising that John Newton, one prominent Abolitionist, was once a slave ship captain.

Part of the refusal of many Liverpool merchants to support abolition of the slave trade in the late eighteenth century was the claim that Liverpool could no longer survive without its profits. Jobs would be lost and businesses bankrupted. However, campaigners such as William Roscoe maintained that Liverpool, and indeed the rest of the country, would cope, and this proved correct; trade continued to expand and flourish in Liverpool for decades after the banning of the trade in 1807.

TRANSPORT AND CONTACTS ON MERSEYSIDE AND BEYOND

Hand in hand with trade and the expansion of Liverpool went an improvement in transport links. Liverpool's location and accessibility had always been important to the growth in its trade, and efforts were made in the seventeenth and eighteenth centuries to maximise the potential of new technologies such as turnpikes, canals and river navigations.

As has been mentioned, the approach roads to Liverpool were in a dire state in the seventeenth century. Their extents nearest the town, such as London Road and Everton Road, were cobbled to help with the packhorse traffic which had been the majority of road users at the time. However, carts were taking over this

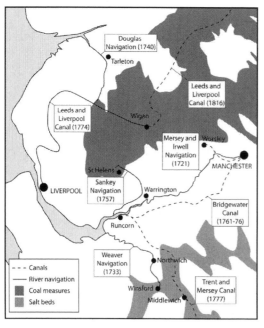

Liverpool found its fortune acting as a transport hub. It sat between the manufacturing centres of Lancashire and Yorkshire on one side and a continental market on the other. Canals were an important route for raw materials as well as finished goods in the years before the railways arrived. The Leeds-Liverpool Canal came right into the centre of town, but even the canals which were scattered further afield played an important role in Liverpool's wealth creation. (After Longmore, J., 'Civic Liverpool', in Belchem, J. (ed), 2006, *Liverpool 800*, Liverpool University Press, Fig. 2.1)

traffic, carrying heavy goods like coal from St Helens, and the cobbled surfaces quickly buckled under this type of weight. Each person in the town was required to give three days' work a year to help keep the roads in good repair. The situation was also helped when the road to Prescot was turned into a turnpike, thus charging road users a toll for passage. When the Douglas Navigation opened (more on this below) this also eased pressure on the town's roads.

Ferries had been a part of the river traffic since the service was begun by medieval monks at Birkenhead Priory, and were affordable at 1*d* per journey (for as many people as you could fit in the ferryboat). But the ability of boats to go further up the Mersey than Warrington was limited, and the poor quality of roads to Manchester meant that only limited amounts of wool, linen or coal could be transported. The Weaver Navigation, a canal built in 1732, was one of the earlier projects with an aim to increase the size of cargoes coming to Liverpool from inland. It improved the transport of coal to the saltworks upriver, and the return of salt down to the port. It also helped stimulate the pottery industry of Staffordshire, which also made use of the channel.

In the middle of the eighteenth century a spate of canal building opened new links to towns across the region and beyond. The Sankey Canal opened in the 1750s, supplying coal to towns and factories. The Bridgewater Canal and the Trent and Mersey Canal opened in the 1760s, both connecting Liverpool with its important neighbour Manchester. The Leeds-Liverpool Canal reached as far as Wigan by 1774, and was finally completed in 1816.

It was becoming obvious that contact with a wide hinterland was crucial to economic success. Merchants had always combined their social lives with professional networking in the coffee houses and trading floors of Liverpool, and over the decades their networks of colleagues, favours and loans spread across the whole country. When Liverpool was founded, residents were granted special privileges, and freedom from certain tolls. In the seventeenth century a system of out-burgesses was begun, with non-residents granted some of these privileges, provided their links were strong enough.

Liverpool was also making sure that it held its own place within the trading networks. It was not just a port but a market for raw materials and finished products. Links expanded with Ireland until the Irish Rebellion of 1641, and Cheshire replaced Brittany, the previous main source, as the top provider of salt. This conscious placement of Liverpool within a stable network of local producers and markets, as well as in the role of port and gateway to the world, set the town up to become the global city of the next century.

CHAPTER 4

LIVING IN LIVERPOOL

Liverpool at the end of the eighteenth century was a neat, semi-rural town, albeit with great ambitions. The built-up area was small, with the Townsend Mill marking the eastern edge and the Wishing Gate windmill its northern. The Wishing Gate mill marked a beautiful spot on the river, where those who remained ashore bid farewell to their loved ones before a voyage.

The new century saw a transformation in Liverpool, from this small town to a giant of industrialised Empire. The arrival of the railway transformed Liverpool physically as well as economically and psychologically. The stations, cuttings and tunnels were to leave lasting marks on the landscape. Other changes would usher Liverpool into a new age: the closing of the Old Dock, the introduction of a police force, gas lighting and focal points like St John's Market were all signs of an expanding town of trade and commerce, and these all arrived in the first three decades of the century.

All this industrialisation and expansion took its toll on the town, however. The building of the Leeds-Liverpool Canal in the Oldfield began the changes which would remove the last vestiges of agriculture from Liverpool. Medieval strips for farming became allotments, market gardens and pigsties, and extraction pits for brick clay. A stretch of residential areas grew up behind the expanding string of docks, densely packed with labourers and their families, particularly to the south of the city centre.

Migrants streamed into Liverpool from other parts of Britain, Europe and all over the Empire. Some were en route or found their way to the Americas, but many stayed, and these new arrivals were easy prey for criminals. In-migration added to the overcrowding problem, and, as we shall see, new projects in health, welfare and philanthropy were established to help deal with these issues.

The nineteenth century also saw two of the most important milestones in the growth of Liverpool. In 1880 another charter was granted, this one giving Liverpool city status. A bishopric, and hence a right to a cathedral, came in the same year. Secondly, in 1895 Liverpool's boundaries were extended to take in parts of West Derby, Wavertree, Toxteth and Walton, bringing the population to nearly 700,000 and creating the suburban landscape we are familiar with today. Within this extended city, zones can be identified based on the characteristic land use: a commercial zone around the old medieval town centre; a philanthropically driven cultural area of grand buildings on Lime Street and around St George's

At the turn of the nineteenth century much of Toxteth and Everton remained rural. This was about to change but, as this engraving shows, Liverpool was still a compact town. The areas just outside the built-up area were already heavily used, by those taking advantage of the fresh air and views, or for washing and drying clothes and linen. (Liverpool Record Office, Liverpool Libraries)

Hall; wealthy housing on Mosslake Fields and later in the suburbs of Anfield and Walton; and industry and less affluent housing in the centre.

With the mass migration of people into Liverpool from all over Britain, drawn by the promise of work or pushed away from the old country by disease or famine, there soon developed a housing crisis. Penniless tenants, unscrupulous landlords and builders, and lack of regulation resulted in a growing inner city slum with a horrific record of health and sanitation. The poorer classes were concentrated in the heart of the city, and as the better central housing was vacated by those escaping to the new suburbs, these buildings were subdivided and multiple-occupied, leading to further overcrowding. It was difficult to convince builders to increase the housing stock: not only were these businesses concentrating on the greater-profit, higher-quality housing for the middle and upper classes on the outskirts of the city, but poverty was increasingly associated with disease and immorality. The question was often raised as to whether the poor even deserved to be helped. This problem would surface a number of times over the coming decades. As Ramsay Muir noted in his 1907 *History of Liverpool*: 'special quarters have developed themselves for the rich, the people of middling fortune, and the poor. That too, perhaps, was inevitable; yet it forms a physical barrier to the growth of the social spirit.'

Trendsetting housing – the rich

While Liverpool had remained a small town, with little more than its original seven streets, all classes of wealth lived in close proximity. Although some streets at this time were wealthier than others, the scale of the town meant that the rich

Until businesses expanded beyond a certain size, it remained convenient for merchants to own a combined home/office/warehouse. Thomas Parr's house on Colquitt Street was a good example, with the taller warehouse (left) being built behind the merchant's home.

rubbed shoulders with the poor. While this may have led to friction between the upper and lower classes, there was little that a Liverpudlian could do – moving to the country meant being away from the cut and thrust of business, and missing out on essential news of shipping, trade and the market.

But as the town grew a divide began to show itself. The wealthier members of society – the merchants in most cases – looked to build themselves new houses on the edges of town. This took them away from the dirty, noisy centre, yet allowed them to socialise amongst themselves in their own polite world of genteel squares, smart terraces and paved roads. Whereas traders had previously found it conveni-ent to build their houses and warehouses into the same city centre building (the classic example being Thomas Parr's 1799 house on Colquitt Street), those who could afford it built new and fashionable houses away from their places of work, on or beyond the edge of the city.

The first area to be developed in this way was the Mosslake Fields, an area now surrounded by the university. Before development there was, as the name sug-gests, a lake in the area, from which a stream flowed down the hill into the Pool. As we have seen, architect Cuthbert Bisbrown had attempted to create a 'New Liverpool' near here in the second half of the eighteenth century and failed. It was in the late eighteenth century and into the nineteenth that the area finally took shape, with the roads beyond the Mosslake Fields being laid out above the town. Even now, just finding its feet as a fashionable and wealthy place to live and do business, Liverpool was consciously aping the likes of Edinburgh, Bath and London, demonstrating its fashion credentials to the scores of travellers it expected as it jostled for its place on the national stage.

Once this pattern had been established, the expansion of Liverpool was char-acterised by the movement of the wealthiest inhabitants out to new suburbs, followed by the middle classes and, finally, the poorest of society, who were left to fill in the gaps vacated by those at the top end of the social scale. This process repeated itself in places ever further from the city centre as the nineteenth cen-tury progressed.

The first new areas to become fashionable after Mosslake Fields and other inner suburbs like Everton and Kirkdale were around the new parks at Sefton, Princes and Newsham. These suburbs were opened up by the development of new transport technologies – trams and trains – which allowed those who could afford it to travel greater distances during their commute. Everton was popular as it provided its inhabitants with impressive views over the Mersey and the Liverpool docklands. As its popularity increased it became a genteel suburb in its own right, a hill crowned with new villas, 'not so densely as to crowd it inconveniently', as James Picton put it in his 1875 history. The villas were dotted along the green lanes which crisscrossed the gently undulating landscape, and the whole of the area retained a rural feel until at least the publication of the First Edition Ordnance Survey map in 1850. From this time onwards, Everton was encroached upon by the expansion of Liverpool to the south and the adjacent area of Anfield became attractive in its place.

The large houses built in Anfield show some of the most explicit attempts to conjure up the rural idyll for which these developments strived. House names like Woodlands, Spring Bank House and Roseneath Cottage evoke not only the sylvan landscapes to which the wealthy aspired, but in their use of 'cottage' and 'lodge' they demonstrated pretensions to both the smaller buildings accompanying lordly estates and the small yet romantic rural labourers' dwellings with which they wished to populate their landscape. But, just like Everton before it, Anfield was soon to be engulfed by the expansion of Liverpool. As terraced roads appeared to the south-east, the market shifted and half-built villa developments were abandoned. The most prestigious street in the area, Anfield Road, was the last to sustain villa development, boosted as it was by the laying out of Stanley Park close by. As new housing projects concentrated more and

As the number of migrants to Liverpool increased, masses of new housing was built to accomodate them. Everton, as an area close to the centre, was soon covered in working-class terraces in a gridiron pattern. Such a pattern expanded across the inner city to nearby areas like Anfield and Walton. (Liverpool North Sheet, from *Plan of Liverpool 1890*)

more on building for the middle classes, the focus for the upper classes moved on again, to West Derby.

West Derby was still entirely rural well into the second half of the nineteenth century. Although the village centre had been in existence, and of some political importance for centuries, it was only in the 1840s that any evidence for modern development can be inferred from Ordnance Survey maps. Like Anfield, West Derby began to be populated by the wealthiest Liverpudlians first. Sandfield Park was developed to strict rules as to what could be built on it, with an annual charge for the upkeep of the park itself. Similarly, Eaton Road, Leyfield Road, Town Row, Hayman's Green, Mill Lane, Yewtree Lane and Deysbrook Lane all developed along similar lines: very large houses in spectacular gardens, set far back from the road. Each house differed from the next, and some had lodges guarding the entrance from the road. By 1900 West Derby took the form of an ancient central village surrounded by a semi-rural landscape of large houses owned by the richest merchants, diplomats and other notable men of Liverpool. But like Anfield, this was to change as housing pressures, and middle-class incomes, increased into the twentieth century.

With the movement of the richest away from the city came a more general awareness of the need for fresh air and space as part of a healthy life. Of course,

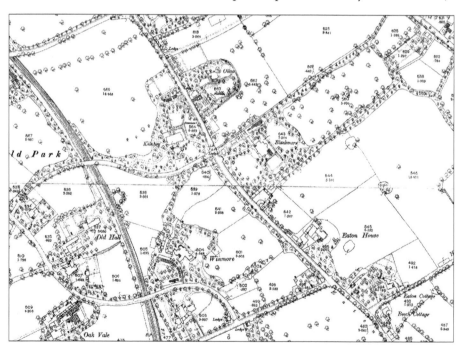

West Derby, being some distance from the town centre, became popular with the wealthiest merchants and diplomats as a suburb to escape to, away from the bustle of business and city centre life. Large villas sprang up across the area, with their owners commuting into town using their own horse and carriage, or later the tram. (Ordnance Survey map of Lancashire and Furness, 1893, 1:2500)

Liverpool in the early nineteenth century provided very little in the way of green space for the majority of its citizens, crowded as they were in the courts (see later in this chapter). An impressive Corporation project to create a series of parks – 'green lungs' for those unable to travel any distance for leisure – ironically gave rise to three further key areas for large houses. Sefton Park, Newsham Park and Stanley Park, as we will see later, were laid out on the edge of the city, on land bought from the Molyneux family of Sefton, or donated by other landowners. Such a project was full of philanthropic intentions, but the method chosen to fund their laying out was to build large, speculative houses on the periphery of the parks. It was hoped that the sale of these villas – large enough to rival some of West Derby's and Anfield's great houses, though placed closer together – would raise the funds necessary for the paths, flowerbeds, lakes and other features envisioned. Even today the large houses which flank Sefton Park and its near neighbour Princes Park survive to tell the tale of this scheme. There are also impressive buildings along West Derby Road, Rocky Lane and Judges Drive around Newsham Park (indeed, the latter road name should be indicative of the kind of residents it hoped to attract). Similar houses around Stanley Park have been swept away by the advance of the city, though there are one or two survivors on Anfield Road.

As the nineteenth century drew to a close, and the twentieth century began, the pattern of newer suburbs for the rich, and the movement of the middling classes out to the commuter areas, continued. As well as the areas looked at here, outlying areas like Seaforth and Childwall also developed into smart settlements for those escaping the city, before in turn being surrounded or replaced by newer, and smaller, properties.

The middling classes move in

Although the business owners and merchants were the wealthiest in Liverpool, the money soon trickled down the ranks, and Liverpool found itself with a large population of clerks, administrative assistants, draughtsmen, customs officers and other skilled workers who also aspired to emulate their superiors – to move out of the dirty town. The same suburbs which had attracted the very richest home owners began to alter in order to cater for these new inhabitants towards the 1860s and '70s. Gradually, the large villas, which had dotted the landscape in previous decades, were replaced with more regular rows of houses.

At first these consisted of terraced villas, of perhaps three storeys, bay windows and a short wall in front to separate it from the pavement, but later these lost favour with developers who built smaller, two-storey terraces, the type which characterise much of Anfield, Tuebrook and parts of Walton today.

This downward trend in house size meant that some more ambitious villa schemes never saw the light of day, or were never completed. They included some of the villa schemes which were intended to fund the laying out of the parks of Newsham and Stanley around 1870. As a result some of the features planned for

Anfield was another suburb to be gradually colonised by rows of terraced housing. Unlike some housing developments, the Anfield roads were built piecemeal, which left odd shapes of land left over when two schemes met. These triangles are preserved in the shape of later roads, like here at Handfield Street and Sockbridge Street. (NMR 20747/60. © English Heritage)

the parks were never added, while other details (such as the lamps on the entrance gates to Newsham Park from Shiel Road) were reduced in size or ornamentation. But this didn't reduce the middle-class wish, like the initial inhabitants of the area, to call upon something of the idyllic, natural and rural. When, for example, in 1865 Breckfield House was demolished to make way for smaller terraces, the roads put in its place were named after Cumbrian Lakes (Windermere, Coniston and Ullswater amongst others).

The trend continued, and uptake of even these terraces slowed in the 1860s and '70s. This resulted in shortened stretches of terraces, or roads containing sections of different-sized houses, as two developers built piecemeal in different styles. As each developer bought up individual plots formerly occupied by a large villa, the field boundaries which were used to define the large properties became fossilised in the road layout of the dense terracing. The gridiron pattern at first meant a relatively regular landscape of roads but, as these were filled in, isolated triangles developed where two builders met at a boundary corner. Imaginative ways were created to deal with these plots, such as building public houses on them, or staggering terraced houses to make best use of the space. By the 1890s almost all the once rural area of Anfield and Breckfield was built on, and the fashionability of the area was largely forgotten.

The final character of the area was one of a sea of terraces, punctuated occasionally by the presence of a public house, the latter built in gaudy glazed brick and tile. Churches and other places of worship were built within the landscape too, some taking up little more than the footprint of the surrounding houses, or ostentatiously rising above the terraced rooftops, signalling their presence loudly to passers-by who might be tempted by the decorated pubs.

Other buildings were constructed in the area to take advantage of the new population centres, or to get around the problems caused by the retreating countryside. Small shops – tobacconists and grocers – came to occupy the main thoroughfares, benefiting from the through traffic and locals looking for food and household items. These houses had living quarters above, much as the merchants of previous generations had lived in houses attached to their places of work. 'Cow houses' – miniature city dairies – looked more like standard terraces, but had access to a yard behind, perhaps taking advantage of the odd triangular spaces left in the centre of a plot. They grew in number to supply fresh milk to local houses as the countryside became too far away to supply perishable goods to the local population.

By the turn of the twentieth century, Liverpool's suburbs had altered completely, driven by the town's growth and the increasing wealth of its citizens. Freed by improvements in road and rail transport, the numbers moving to the edge of town increased, until places like Anfield, Breckfield and Walton consisted of a sea of regular terraced houses. But despite the relatively high density of housing at this point, compared to what it once was, the terraces were of good quality and were comfortable. Conditions were much better than those in the city centre.

Court housing and poverty

For the majority of the poor, who could not afford to escape even to the innermost suburbs, living conditions were harsh, with families squeezed into extremely low-quality housing by population pressure and unscrupulous developers. The meanest houses were barely fit for human habitation, and the phrase 'court house' became a byword for the squalor in which too many Liverpudlians were trapped.

Thrown up for the lowest cost possible, court houses consisted of a narrow yard less than 4m wide with back-to-back housing on either side. The entrance at one end of the courtyard was through a narrow passage from the main road, while at the other end of the yard was a communal cesspit, cleaned irregularly by a 'nightsoil man' who collected the waste and took it to the town middens. The only source of running water would have been a standpipe in the road or the yard, shared with the other families and running into the same cesspit as the rest of the court's waste. This was nowhere near enough sanitation for the numbers of people likely to be occupying the building, and water-borne diseases like cholera and typhoid were rife.

The houses themselves were poorly built, some with walls of only half a brick's thickness. Two or three above-ground storeys were two rooms deep, meaning the back rooms got only as much light and fresh air as filtered through the front rooms. The cellars were also occupied as pressures on the housing stock increased, and this accommodation was even worse than its neighbours. The floors were

Court houses were damp, cramped, poor-quality buildings with too many families squeezed in. Disease was rife, and some of the first efforts to demolish slum houses focussed on these buildings, which became notorious examples of inner-city deprivation. (Ordnance Survey map of Lancashire and Furness, 1891, 1:500)

of packed earth and the rooms were dim and damp, without even windows to complement the meagre supply of air and light coming into the subterranean entrance. The rooms on all floors were barely 6ft in height, around 12ft square. These cramped conditions were made worse with the number of families forced through poverty to live together. Sometimes two or even more families could be found in a single one of these dismal rooms. Added to this, a family at the time might have contained three or more children, with the parents and grandparents living under one roof. In the middle of the century Dr William Henry Duncan, the Medical Officer for Health, estimated that half of the working classes lived in these conditions, with St Paul's, Exchange and Vauxhall having the highest density of this housing type.

Slums outside the city centre

Although courts were predominantly a feature of the city centre and purpose-built by unscrupulous developers, courts and other slums could also be found in the inner suburbs such as Walton. Many of these houses had their origins in a time when large Georgian houses were being vacated as merchants moved further into the countryside in the nineteenth century. Speculative landlords bought up these large city dwellings and divided them up for renting out to the poor. Housing was in great demand at this time, and so the available stock was soon filled.

Poor migrants from England and other parts of Britain and Ireland were flooding into the city. Lacking more than a very basic means to set themselves up in their new home, these people had to find solutions to both the problems of homelessness and joblessness as close to the centre as possible. Commuting in from West Derby or Garston was out of the question, and so the demand for central housing was maintained even as stocks were running short. Thus working-class housing spread into Kirkdale, Bootle, Everton and similar areas where a commute to casual dock work was still possible on foot.

Court houses were the very lowest end of the scale, but were found together with similarly drab dwellings as back-to-backs and cheap terraced housing. The roads themselves varied in width: some were respectable while others were barely more than back-alleys, crammed in to maximise housing space. The overall pattern though was of a dense mass, a gridiron of perpendicular roads running off the main thoroughfares like Scotland Road in north Liverpool and Princes Road in the south.

The publication of Edwin Chadwick's *The Sanitary Condition of the Working Population of Great Britain* in 1842 helped identify the role played by housing quality in the spread of disease. Houses built so close together, and sharing such meagre sanitation, were breeding grounds for germs, rats and other disease carriers. Cholera outbreaks in 1832 and 1848 led to the 1848 Public Health Act, which attempted to improve the sanitary conditions in the towns and cities of Britain. Liverpool soon banned court housing in the wake of the Act, and at the same time set up a Health Board to oversee improvements. However, widespread examples of court housing could still be seen in Liverpool until the 1930s, with the last two remaining examples (now belonging to the Liverpool School of Tropical Medicine) situated at 35 and 37 Pembroke Place. Much of this road pattern was removed as part of continued slum clearance projects in the twentieth century, but the names of many survive in truncated or newly curving roads in the positions once occupied by court houses.

SOLVING LIVERPOOL'S HOUSING PROBLEM

The housing stock itself was a central part of the overcrowding problem: in 1919 there were 2,770 back-to-back tenements left in the city, despite efforts to clear away the worst of the nineteenth-century slums. Even as late as 1955 the Medical Officer for Health counted 88,000 unfit dwellings in the city, basing these judgements on a lack of amenities, or on houses which caused ill health (for example if the building lacked stability, had little or no natural light, or suffered from problems of damp, insufficient drainage or absence of cooking facilities). Ten years later, 78,000 of these residences were still standing.

Tuberculosis, a disease closely associated with poverty, remained high in Liverpool even after dramatic drops in its frequency across the rest of the country. The central and riverside areas of Liverpool remained the worst-affected right through from the Victorian period to 1935. Even when the Corporation built new tenements the health problems continued, demonstrating that it was not only housing, but poverty itself which was the problem. Something more than a mere increase in housing stock was needed to cure the woes of inner-city slums.

The obstacle faced by anyone in the nineteenth century who wanted to address disease, overcrowding and poor housing was one of apathy, or outright opposition. Hugh Shimmin, a prominent voice in the press, was just one voice suggesting that many of the working class were lazy, and undeserving of any help at all. Despite this, efforts were made at a civic level to improve the living conditions of the working class. The 1842 Building Act allowed the Corporation to enforce basic standards of housing, and the 1846 Liverpool Sanitary Act gave the Corporation the power to close the worst of the cellar dwellings, and introduce the country's first Medical Officer for Health, Dr William H. Duncan. Dr Duncan led the Health Committee to inspect cellars and other dwellings, and had the power to throw people out of their homes if conditions were bad enough. However, because these people were not re-homed by the Committee, this hardly led to an improvement in the situation.

Further legislation followed the previous Acts. In 1864 the Sanitary Amendment Act laid the foundations for later housing schemes, and the national Housing Acts of 1866, 1875 and 1890 were attempts to improve the minimum quality of housing. The Insanitary Property and Artizan's Dwelling Committee oversaw the buying up of property, which was only resold to landlords on the assumption that the very worst of the houses would be demolished.

The Labouring Classes Dwelling Houses Act of 1866 had been the first Act of Parliament to allow the social provision of housing. St Martin's Cottages, opened on Ashfield Street in 1869, were the country's first council houses. However, even though they had been designed for the poorest people, the rents were too high

Liverpool City Council pioneered the provision of social housing. St Martin's Cottages were the very first of these, situated between Sylvester Street and Ashfield Street in Vauxhall. (Trustees of National Museums Liverpool)

for this sector of society to afford, particularly those who had been thrown out of the slums under recent legislation. Instead these houses were occupied by the slightly more well off – railway workers, shipbuilders and metal workers.

These local Acts and measures were better able to deal with the problems from a financial and bureaucratic point of view, but they were limited in scope as they did not demand the construction of any new affordable housing to replace that which they cleared. In this case, slum clearance often actually made the problem worse – in the 1890s more houses were demolished than were built, and where building did take place, it concentrated in the wealthy suburbs, where more profits were to be made by developers.

Council building schemes

Towards the end of the nineteenth century it was clear that legislation and the private sector had failed to solve the housing crisis, and so the council began to take more direct action to alleviate population pressure. Despite the limitations of the St Martin's Cottages scheme, more council houses were built and, by 1919, 2,895 dwellings were owned by the local authority, around 12 per cent of all such housing in Britain at the time. After the First World War 35,000 further council homes were built. It has been suggested that Liverpool had been successful in its aims to help the 'poorest poor' by this time, but many of even the earliest new houses, in Huyton and Norris Green for example, were too far from the town centre, and built without basic facilities such as local shops, transport and places for children to play. Such a pattern was to be repeated later in the century.

Post-Second World War schemes

The Second World War interrupted these projects, and little more was done to build new homes until the Mersey Plan of 1944. The Plan resumed house building with greater vigour and a higher level of 'decantation' of people from the inner-city areas to the outskirts.

The 1954 Housing Repair and Rents Act had allowed the council to take decisive action to combat the problem of poor-quality housing. Instead of relying on the private sector to meet the housing demands of the poorer citizens, and at the same time help clear the city of its slums, the council could take things into its own hands, having been given the power to demolish sub-standard housing themselves, judging such dwellings on whether they met eight requirements for fitness.

A Labour Council came to power in 1955 with Jack Braddock at its head. Braddock was determined to solve the housing problem, and about a third of the city's 47 square miles eventually succumbed to the wrecking ball. The pace of clearance accelerated in 1964 when Braddock's successor, William Sefton, started a more structured renewal scheme. The national government had established a National Building Agency which was to examine current schemes across the country and overhaul them, and the local council was determined to make the most of this opportunity.

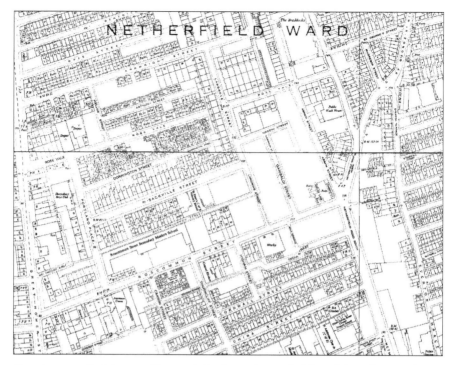

Slum clearance efforts increased in pace during the post-war rebuilding of the mid-twentieth century. Prefabricated concrete was becoming a popular building material, allowing towers to be put up quickly to rehome those whose homes were destroyed in the Blitz or by clearance schemes. Vast areas of the inner city were left empty for years, the ghosts of former streets traced on maps from the era. (Ordnance Survey map of Cheshire, 1958-61, 1:2500)

It was calculated that both green and brownfield sites were needed to build enough homes for everyone, finding that 148,000 of the people who needed rehousing could not be fitted into the existing city boundary. The solution was to obtain sites outside the boundary where thousands of new homes could be constructed. The powers necessary to carry out these plans, allowing the local authority to build shops, houses and other such amenities, had come in the form of the 1936 Liverpool Corporation Act. In the wake of the Act the council was allowed to buy, sell and develop land, and so sites were acquired by the council at Cantril Farm, Huyton and Speke.

Model housing estates were built at these locations in the 1960s, and by the time this process was nearly complete between 160,000 and 200,000 people had been moved to the council-owned estates of Kirkby, Halewood and Speke, plus housing at Croxteth, Cantril Farm (later renamed Stockbridge Village), Huyton and Netherley. As an example of the impact these new residents had on the existing settlements, in 1921 Speke had a population of 3,666, which had grown to 27,000 by 1961.

Liverpool's response to the continued housing problem was to build social housing more enthusiastically than any other town in England (and it clashed with Margaret Thatcher's government in the 1980s for this very reason). While this can be seen as pioneering in many respects, the results of development left a lot to be desired.

Problems with the council schemes

Many of the problems associated with the building of council houses were due to the sheer number of dwellings that were needed. The two sides of the issue were that both the number of houses that needed clearing and also the number of new properties to replace them were underestimated.

New building suffered from a lack of planning. At first, and based on the council's own calculations, five-storey tenements were considered the maximum height necessary to meet demand. However, this proved optimistic and, following examples seen in the USA, the restriction was abandoned in favour of tower blocks up to fifteen storeys high.

Only once people had been rehoused was it discovered that high-rise living was not to everyone's taste. Partly this was due to the lack of amenities, but also the isolation of living dozens of floors up. Residents were separated from each other by walkways, separate roadways for vehicles, and bland open spaces between the buildings. People's homes were far from the streets, where once

In addition to the new tower blocks of Everton and other parts of the city, housing estates on the outskirts were built to take thousands of people 'decanted' from the centre of Liverpool. These were located in locations which were attractive to industry, and where such industry could establish itself and expand, such at Speke, Aintree and Kirkby. This aerial photo has been marked up by city engineers with the routes of proposed new roads. (EPW023559. © English Heritage (Aerofilms Collection))

their houses would have fronted straight onto the pavement. Even everyday travel (to shops and work) required the use of the mere handful of buses which were available, raising the cost of living. After only a decade 'four out of five tenants on the [Netherley] estate desperately wanted to leave' (*Liverpool Echo*, 25 May 1979).

There was little planning to the process of demolition. Plots were destroyed whenever they became vacant, fragmenting large residential areas of the city for decades. Scotland Road itself was almost completely demolished from the Queensway Tunnel to Harebell Street, and yet Liverpool's courts were still being demolished in the 1960s. Parts of Everton and Kirkdale waited to be cleared well into the 1980s. Old communities were torn apart and sent to separate towns and estates. Even today, as told in books like *The Lost Tribe of Everton and Scottie Road*, a nostalgia still pervades those who lived in roads now transformed or destroyed by twentieth-century clearance and redevelopment. One group of residents attempted to save themselves from this fate when they tried to buy derelict land and rebuild their own community on it. The group, from Vauxhall in north Liverpool, formed a cooperative, the Eldonian Village, in order to buy land on the closed Tate & Lyle sugar refinery and build their own new homes. However, the council – dominated by the Militant tendency – refused to give them planning permission on the ideological grounds that all housing policy should be directed from the centre, and that any support for the scheme would take funds from council projects. This unwillingness of the council to shift from their ambitious centralised housing scheme meant that the group had to wait several more years before their dreams could be realised.

Alongside project-level issues, there were problems with the buildings themselves. The quality of the new high-rises and tenements was low. Walls were thin, the very architecture was cramped and repetitive, and the buildings were prone to damp. Some blocks had such short life spans that they were being demolished less than twenty years after they were built – at the same time that the slums they were designed to be replacing were still being pulled down.

CHANGING HOUSING: TWENTIETH-CENTURY SUBURBS

As Liverpool's growth exploded in the late nineteenth century and into the twentieth, the council saw the need to provide not only homes for the 'poorest poor', but also infrastructure to the private developments in the suburbs. With this in mind the rural lanes across Anfield and Walton-on-the-Hill were widened and straightened and, around the beginning of the twentieth century, city engineer J.A. Brodie constructed Queens Drive, a visionary thoroughfare which opened up the edges of the city to massive private and Corporation development in the years which followed.

In the period between the wars, and particularly in the 1930s, house buying outstripped renting for the first time in Liverpool. This was helped by falling

The expansion of Liverpool in the twentieth century included new and spacious suburbs for the increasing numbers of those who wished to escape the city centre. Norris Green was one area where building projects placed schemes wholesale across the landscape. These distinctive curved roads are easy to spot on modern maps, and were even more obvious features when first built. (EPW003058. © English Heritage (Aerofilms Collection))

prices and an increase in incomes, allowing more people to consider home ownership and fund the deposit and mortgage required. As a result, many more people on middling incomes could afford to live further out from the city centre, and the outlying regions of Liverpool were developed into suburbs to take advantage of this. In fact, it became cheaper for those in the skilled middle classes to pay a deposit and mortgage than it was to rent from either the Corporation or a private landlord. Following the rise in demand, most homes built from the 1930s onwards were intended for private buyers, rather than as social housing or the rental market.

The reasons behind the emergence of the twentieth-century suburbs were similar to those of the previous century: people who could do so moved to the outskirts to escape the crowded, noisy and dirty city centre. However, unlike the nineteenth-century piecemeal development in places like Anfield, these large new suburbs were planned and executed wholesale across large swathes of the landscape, with no need to respect existing field boundaries. The shapes of whole estates like Norris Green are therefore easy to spot on a map, with their regular curving roads laid out to one overarching plan. Wavertree Garden Suburb is a special case, with 360 houses built between 1910 and 1915 by a partnership called

Liverpool Garden Suburb Tenants Ltd. This was a miniature version of the model villages of the nineteenth century (of which the closest was Port Sunlight on the Wirral), filled with a variety of housing architecture based on the Arts and Crafts movement. The density of housing was deliberately kept low, as a reaction to the overcrowding which was going on in the city centre at the time. The residents even drew up a 'constitution', dictating how the community was to operate. Such actions are not surprising considering the conditions experienced by fellow Liverpudlians in other areas of the city.

The inner suburbs were beginning to suffer. Although they had been well-provisioned with small shopping arcades and even local dairies and food producers, there was no room to expand. Car ownership increased over the twentieth century, both in the modern suburbs and the more central areas like Anfield and Walton. This freed people both to commute further to work, and to travel longer distances for shopping and leisure. The smaller-scale suburban businesses could not compete with out-of-town shopping malls or retail parks, and a decline set in. A knock-on effect was to drive more and more people to move to the more spacious of the suburbs, further fuelling the sense of abandonment that places such as Everton and Walton experienced after the Second World War.

Over the course of the nineteenth and twentieth centuries Liverpool had progressed from a small town, via a cramped Victorian metropolis into a sprawling modern conurbation. The divisions between the wealthier and the poorer inhabitants had increased, both financially and geographically, and this was reflected in the housing stock. Efforts were made to improve or remove the worst of the slums, while new areas of the city were engulfed by ever-increasing suburban development. The landscape of modern Liverpool contains the combined results of the many housing trends which swept across the city, from the Georgian terraces of the Mosslake Fields, through the inner-city terraces of Toxteth, Walton and Anfield, the inter-war semi-detached houses of West Derby, Allerton and Childwall, the modern suburbs at Croxteth and the council estates of Kirkby, Halewood and Knowsley. But even if housing shaped the bulk of Liverpool's urban landscape, it was innovation in transport – for Liverpudlians and for trade – which really enabled the speed and shape of Liverpool's expansion across the last 200 years.

CHAPTER 5

DOCKS, THE PORT AND INDUSTRY

Liverpool and its docklands have been inseparable since the construction of the Old Dock in 1702. As one developed in a certain direction, the other adapted along with it. The shape of the docklands owes much to the landscape of Liverpool, both the natural coastline as well as the built-up urban landscape inland, meaning that it was always cheaper to build new docks to the north and south of existing areas, even though this meant moving the actual activity of loading and unloading further and further from the business district and the offices of the merchants.

Liverpool was little more than a medieval fishing town before it found its vocation as a trade and transport hub, and from then on it rose to become a central force in the fortunes of the British Empire and the wealth of the country. The entire process was set in motion almost 200 years earlier, when the Corporation bet the entire estate on a ludicrously ambitious project to build an enclosed wet dock. Liverpool was still in its infancy, and only gradually built up its trade routes, but by the beginning of the nineteenth century, the city was coming into its own as an entrepreneurial and industrious centre of exchange. Unfortunately, when trade moved away from the west coast to the south-east of England in the twentieth century, Liverpool was left with little to fall back on. Despite valiant attempts to rekindle the local economy and introduce new industries to south Lancashire in the early to mid-twentieth century, Liverpool was to suffer an extended depression until the eve of the Millennium.

THE NINETEENTH CENTURY: LIVERPOOL'S POTENTIAL

One of the Liverpool's strengths was that it became a general cargo port, unlike other more specialised British ports such as Newcastle (coal) or Swansea (copper). From its earliest history, Liverpool played the role of a transport hub, and by the end of the eighteenth century it was at the crossroads between canal and river routes.

The city's geography was of particular help, with the town sitting in a sheltered position on a large river, the gateway to the coast for large areas of south Lancashire, Cheshire, North Wales and the Midlands. It was a short hop to the Isle of Man and Ireland, and would later on be the main western port for departures to the Americas. Once Liverpool had cemented its place at the centre of trading networks across Britain and beyond, there was little to stop its growth.

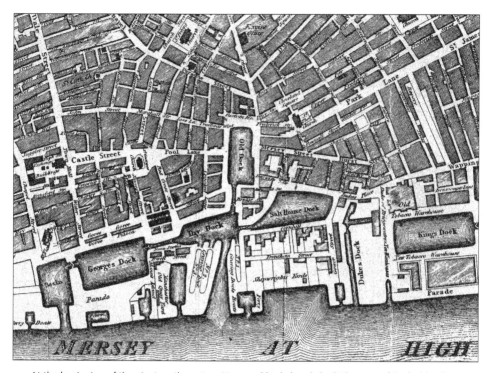

At the beginning of the nineteenth century Liverpool had already built the core of its docklands. The Old Dock was still in use, and had been expanded into a small network of basins. This map also shows the Customs House, Exchange and the Excise Office – all crucial buildings in the operation of a port. (Extract from Kaye's Map of Liverpool, 1910)

Liverpool was not just a town with a port. The town *was* the port, and vice versa. The entire waterfront was lined with docks, and warehouses occupied a wide strip behind them. Workshops clustered in the back streets – mini-industries which served the ship owners by making and repairing ropes, sails and other paraphernalia. The Town Hall itself was also the Exchange, and the Customs House, opened in 1839 on the site of the filled-in Old Dock, was the centre of excise collection in the centre of the town. The roads nearby all led down to it as they had done to the dock on which it sat.

The entrepreneurial spirit of the town's merchants also played a part: new developments and markets were exploited whenever possible. The South American market was one such new destination, after the independence wars of the nineteenth century, as were India and China following the disbanding of the East India Company's monopoly. With the introduction of steam Liverpool ships more often traded with the Mediterranean, and with the Crimean War many steamships were chartered from Liverpool builders to aid the war effort. Finally, after the American Civil War the American fleet practically disappeared from the Atlantic, and Liverpool boats filled the gap left by them.

JESSE HARTLEY AND NEW DOCK TECHNOLOGY

Liverpool maintained its competitiveness through its technological and architectural innovations. Older docks became obsolete as newer and larger ships no longer fitted through the lock gates. The Old Dock (opened in 1715) was still in use up to 1826, but already in 1811 an Act of Parliament had granted the Corporation permission to fill it in. This finally happened in 1827, ushering in a new phase in the development of the Mersey Docks. A new Customs House, the fifth for the town and designed by John Foster the Younger, was built on top of the filled in Old Dock, taking up a prime central position in the midst of the docklands. Afterwards, new and larger docks were built, avoiding the cramped city centre by being constructed on reclaimed land to the north and south.

One of the most important moments in the history of Liverpool's docks was the appointment in 1824 of Jesse Hartley as Civil Engineer and Superintendent of the Concerns of the Dock Estate. Hartley's first job was on the Brunswick Dock and Half-tide basin, both completed in 1832, and for the next thirty years he redeveloped Liverpool's entire dock estate. In addition to adding 10 miles of quayside, he oversaw the building of a railway system to help transport material for new docks. His 'cyclopean' architectural style (huge irregular stone blocks closely bonded) characterises the docks even to this day, and he more than quadrupled the acreage of the Merseyside docklands during his lifetime.

Hartley was at the forefront of new technologies, and made every effort to incorporate his own and other's innovations into dock and warehouse construction. The Albert Dock of 1845 was one of Hartley's finest works, and displays some of his revolutionary ideas. Contracted to build new warehouses on the south side of the Salthouse Dock he first built models at the Trentham Street Dockyard nearby to test his designs. He closely specified the quality of bricks which were

Jesse Hartley was an innovative architect and engineer, and the Albert Dock rightly stands as a monument to his technique and skill. Easily visible are the 'cyclopean' architecture which used large blocks of stone, plus the arches which would have held cranes for pulling cargoes ashore, and the tough stone corners which protected the building from damage caused by heavily laden trolleys of cargo knocking into it.

to be used, established his own stone quarry in Kirkmabreck, Scotland, and built the *Oak*, a coaster (a shallow-hulled merchant vessel) to bring the stone from this quarry to Liverpool.

The Albert Dock is Hartley's most famous legacy. Among his breakthroughs was the use of sheet metal for the roof. This design could withstand fire for 40 minutes unchecked, and was influential in future developments of the dock estate, as well as the designs for fireproof mills throughout Lancashire. The dock was one of the first in the world to have warehouses right at the water's edge. Speed was always of the essence, and as a wet dock, ships in the Albert Dock could berth at high tide, unload straight into the warehouse, and leave as soon as the water level in the river allowed.

The warehouses themselves were fireproof: iron columns held up stone floors, and the building was capped with an iron roof. In addition, the Albert Dock warehouses were 'bonded' warehouses, which meant that customs dues were not paid when cargo moved between boat and quay. Instead they were only paid when stock was moved out of the warehouse, so further decreasing the time a ship needed to wait in port. Keys to the warehouse were kept by a representative of the Crown and huge amounts of goods might be stored in the many bonded warehouses on the Mersey at any one time. The continued use of the warehouses in new developments (see later) is a testament to Hartley's ability to create practical and yet long-lasting buildings. More docks in Liverpool followed the example, with the warehouses at Stanley and Wapping Docks also built as bonded storage. The colossal Tobacco Warehouse at Stanley Dock (built 1897–1901) was the largest in the world, exemplifying Liverpool's place within the global trade network.

NINETEENTH-CENTURY DOCK EXPANSION

The nineteenth century was a crucial period for the Liverpool docklands. By 1800 the town had already built the world's first commercial wet dock, but if it was to stay at the forefront of world trade it could not afford to rest on these laurels. The Corporation, then still owning the dock estate, began a process of building new docks and enlarging existing ones. This continued through the century, with the town spending millions of pounds to keep trade flowing, and to adapt to the changes in shipping brought about by the Industrial Revolution.

1709–1825: Corporation control

The Corporation remained in control of the estate until 1825. In this time it built Canning (1813) and Princes Dock (1822), removing the old fort at the north end of town to build the latter, and replacing it with a fortified battery at the north end of Clarence Dock. The Corporation also enlarged Queens Dock, and altered and re-opened Georges Dock in the centre of the estate to bring it up to modern standards.

New basins had been added to the dock system since the first opened in 1715, but the nineteenth century saw an explosion of new additions, and remains the greatest period of dockland expansion in Liverpool's history. It also saw a number of docks being reshaped or expanded to take the form we recognise today. (After Patmore, J.A. & Hodgkiss, A.G., *Merseyside in Maps*, p38 Fig. A, 1970, Longman with additions)

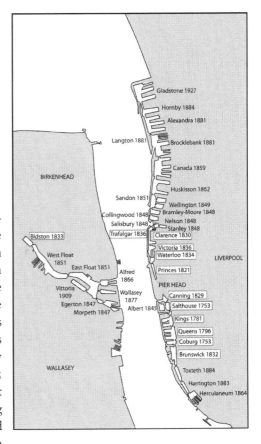

Gladstone 1927
Hornby 1884
Alexandra 1881
Langton 1881
Brocklebank 1881
Canada 1859
BIRKENHEAD
Huskisson 1862
Sandon 1851
Wellington 1849
Collingwood 1848
Bramley-Moore 1848
Salisbury 1848
Nelson 1848
Stanley 1848
Bidston 1833
Trafalgar 1836
Clarence 1830
Victoria 1836
West Float 1851
Waterloo 1834
LIVERPOOL
East Float 1851
Alfred 1866
Princes 1821
Vittoria 1909
Wallasey 1877
PIER HEAD
Egerton 1847
Albert 1845
Canning 1829
Morpeth 1847
Salthouse 1753
Kings 1781
Queens 1796
Coburg 1753
Brunswick 1832
WALLASEY
Toxteth 1884
Harrington 1883
Herculaneum 1864

1825–1857: Dock Committee control

An Act of 1811 had created a separate Dock Committee of twenty-one members and given them their own seal and budget. This was to deal with accusations that the Corporation were too self-serving. However, there were still no rate-paying members of this committee, and it was still seen as unrepresentative of the vast majority of users of the dock. Therefore in 1825 another Act was passed whereby eight members were added to the existing twenty-one, all of which were elected by ratepayers. There were still thirteen town councillors on the committee, and the Council still elected the chair. Whether or not this change was the key factor in the future fortunes of the docks is hard to say, but it did usher in an era when there was an explosion of dock construction.

In the latter part of the 1820s Canning and Clarence Docks were constructed. Brunswick was not far behind, a specialist timber dock where the quays sloped down to the water to better allow the cargo to be unloaded. Brunswick was on the site of Jackson's Dam, used to power a watermill in Liverpool's early history. The later 1830s also saw the appearance of Trafalgar, Victoria (both 1836) and Waterloo Docks (1834). These three were groundbreaking: they were the first docks on the river to align their shorter sides with the riverbank. These were the early days of steamships, and it became more important to maximise the length of quays for loading and unloading, in contrast to the plans for previous docks for which water area was of prime importance. By arranging the docks in this way Hartley maximised quay space in the minimum amount of riverbank. Thus as much space as possible was preserved for future dock development.

Meanwhile steam technology was having an effect on the southern docklands. Coburg Dock opened in the early 1840s, with the intention of catering for steam ships. As early steam technology involved the use of side paddles, the gates of

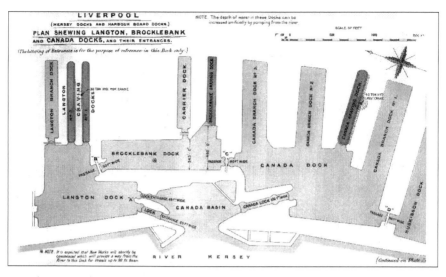

An ambitious port had to keep up with new technological developments if it was to stay at the
forefront of trade. The first steam-powered ships were paddle steamers, with wheels making
them much wider than previous boats. For this reason dock gates were made much wider than
they had been, although the rapid replacement of paddle with screw-driven ships quickly made
these adjustments obsolete. (Liverpool – Langton, Brocklebank and Canada Docks, from the
Dock Book, June 1909, British Admiralty)

Coburg were over 70ft wide, with more than 4 acres of water. The dock provided direct access from the river at first, and was developed from the basin of
Brunswick Dock which had been open for almost a decade already. Expansion
in the southern docks continued with the construction of Toxteth Dock to
the south of Brunswick in 1842. In the same year the Salthouse Dock and the
Canning Dock were altered and enlarged respectively, again adapting to the
changing needs of shipping.

   Liverpool's reputation for dock technology was cemented in 1846 with the
opening of the Albert Dock, Jesse Hartley's enduring masterpiece. Duke's Dock,
an old basin to the south of Albert and opened in 1773, was now in the way of
expansion, and was only suitable for river craft. Therefore Wapping Dock was
built inland of Kings Dock, connected to the Salthouse Dock via a cut behind
the obstructing Dukes. This grand scheme required the Dock Committee to buy
over £300,000 of property to make space by demolition, and also to move the
road Wapping further east. The road now sits on the site of the Salt House which
gave its name to the nearby dock.

   The year 1848 saw an explosion in the size of the dock estate, with the opening of Collingwood, Stanley (the only dock built on the land side of the dock
road since the Old Dock), Nelson, Bramley-Moore and Salisbury. Salisbsury
Dock included the Victoria Tower, a massive clock tower which let sailors set
their watches as they passed into the Irish Sea, and also warned them of impend-
ing weather and tide changes by the ringing of a bell. Based on a drawing by

Philip Hardwick, it is a classic of Hartley construction with its cyclopean granite masonry. Pevsner called it 'all ham' with its castellations and parapet, but acknowledged that it was typical of the pride and boastfulness of the times. Another key feature of the dock was the lack of an outer basin. While it had long been the case that ships needed calm waters to sail into before docking, the newer steam-powered ships didn't need this luxury.

As the 1850s dawned further construction got under way. In 1850 the Wellington Dock opened, with Sandon following a year later, and Huskisson the year after that. In 1851 the Manchester Dock, which wasn't connected to the rest of the system but rather opened directly into the River Mersey, was purchased, having been used until then by the Shropshire Union Railways and Canal Company and the Great Western Railway as a depot for imports being transferred to rail. In 1853 Clarence Dock was enlarged, and a year later a new fort and barracks were built on the northwest corner of Huskisson Dock to replace the one demolished on Hogs Hey Nook to make way for Collingwood Dock. Just before the Mersey Docks and Harbour Board took over the running of the docklands, Wapping Dock was opened in 1855. In the same year the important city centre Salthouse Dock was enlarged again, and in 1856 Queens Dock was deepened and two half-tide docks added to it.

1857 onwards: Mersey Docks and Harbour Board

As the 1850s wore on, the Liverpool Corporation came under increasing pressure from Manchester merchants, dock users and Parliament to give up some control of the docks, as their monopoly was being used unfairly to benefit themselves. Thus in 1858 responsibility for the River Mersey and the Port of Liverpool passed from the Corporation-controlled Dock Committee to the newly formed Mersey Docks and Harbour Board (MDHB).

Of the Board, twenty-four members were elected by the rate-payers (the dock users) while the remainder were nominated by the government on behalf of others' interests, such as those of Birkenhead and Manchester. While this institution was still the subject of criticism from those who saw it as a monopolistic giant, it had the freedom to plough forward with improvements and expansions of the dock estate, where other ports had to deal with a variety of interests such as private dock owners and railway companies. It could also be seen as the moment when the administration of the docks separated from that of the city. Thus the interests of the two became conflicting and separate, the representatives of one having no interests in the other. What is certain is that, in this era, more time was spent expanding current docks than building new ones, although additions to the dock count were certainly made.

Soon after the MDHB came into existence it built the Canada Dock at the far north end of the city, and the Coburg Dock was expanded by breaking into the Union Dock. Brunswick was enlarged for a second time the same year (1858). Two years later Huskisson was extended, with a new branch added in 1861. Brocklebank Dock, also part of the northern docklands, was opened, being known as Canada Half Tide dock until 1879. Herculaneum, to the south of the city centre, opened in 1866. In 1868 a half-tide basin was added to Princes, while Waterloo Dock was enlarged into the two basins it occupies today: East and West. When being enlarged, Waterloo was adapted for a specialist role in the corn trade, with cranes and other machinery suited to this job being installed.

The last thirty years of the nineteenth century saw a great programme of enlarging and improving the existing docks. In 1871 Brocklebank was enlarged, and a second branch was added to Huskisson in 1872. Brunswick got its first branch in 1878, and was then enlarged for the third time in 1889. Herculaneum was enlarged, and a branch added, in 1881, while Huskisson was altered in 1896 and 1897. Canada Dock was enlarged to allow the wide paddle steamers in 1896, but already this was the age of the rear steam screw, and the extra width was quickly obsolete.

New docks built in this era were, in the north, Langton (1879), the massive Alexandra with its three branches which gave more quay space (1880) and Hornby Dock and its branch to the north of Alexandra (1884). In the south, Harrington (1883) and Toxteth (1888) appeared towards the last decade of the nineteenth century. A new Union Dock (replacing that which became part of the Coburg Dock in 1858) was opened in 1889.

The Docks at the end of the nineteenth century

Although Liverpool had actively chased an increasing level of trade from the moment it opened the Old Dock in 1709, the nineteenth century saw a massive increase in the dock estate. Profits ballooned, as did the physical size of the estate, rising from 46 acres of water and 2 miles of quayside in 1825 to 192 acres of water and 15 miles of quay in 1857. And even though the number of vessels docking fell from 10,000 to 6,000 in the last thirty years of the century, the size of the ships now pulling into port increased by such a large amount that total tonnage went up by 66 per cent.

Clearly Liverpool's efforts to keep up with the times had paid off. The coming of the steam ships had meant a complete reconstruction of the docks they used, but Liverpool never failed to expand basins where necessary, or install systems adapted to the particular cargoes coming in. As the century drew to a close this process continued. The southern system had been vastly enlarged between 1881 and 1888, and the northern system was completely reconstructed between 1890 and 1906. The latter was done to accommodate the vast American liners which had previously used (and outgrown) the once cutting-edge technology of Alexandra and Hornby docks nearby.

In addition to the docks themselves, from 1890 serious and continued efforts were made to dredge the mouth of the Mersey. The merchants of Liverpool knew well the fate of Chester, where the silting of the Dee had made it impassable to larger boats (so freeing Liverpool to succeed its old rival). The ever-increasing size of ships coming down the Mersey required that this be done, and even the £1 million annual cost of this process was an essential investment to keep Liverpool's deep water passage and maintain its position at the forefront of global trade.

BUSINESS PREMISES IN CENTRAL VICTORIAN LIVERPOOL

Business in Liverpool naturally began as a very centralised collection of offices and workshops. Merchants in the eighteenth century lived close, or even next door, to their warehouses for security and practical reasons. These houses were in turn close to the Town Hall and Exchange, with the most expensive properties being those nearest to these important buildings. Liverpool was expanding in the nineteenth century, however, and with the increasing overcrowding the richer members of society looked to the rural fringes of the town to build larger houses. Even those who could not afford to move out of the centre had to live further away from their place of work, in a town centre which was eventually dominated by the offices of hundreds of different companies, rather than any housing. It was no longer economically sound to build a house and storage room in the same building. As the business district thus grew larger, certain industries clustered their office premises together in different parts of Liverpool, to take advantage of certain land prices or simply to benefit from working near each other.

Shipping companies understandably clustered around the Pier Head, James Street and Water Street. From here they were within easy walking distance of

Offices were not merely a place of work. They told fellow Liverpudlians – especially other traders – how prestigious your company was. Speculative offices were built by architects who aimed to impress. The India Buildings were one such development, designed to hold more than one company who all wanted to use the space. The current buildings, designed by Herbert Rowse, replaced another smaller structure of the same name.

The Liver Building is perhaps the most famous building associated with a company. However, the office was inhabited by several companies, the rent from which allowed the Royal Liver Group to build a much larger building than they could afford to any other way. This prestigious waterfront site was completed with the addition of the headquarters of the Cunard Line, and the offices of the Mersey Docks and Harbour Board.

their own ships coming into dock (a particular advantage to the messengers and couriers who rushed around the town passing on news and communications). Most of these companies occupied a floor or two in speculative office blocks like the India and Tower Buildings, but the most successful companies felt the need for their own dedicated offices to show just how prestigious they were. These top companies included the White Star Line (with their distinctive headquarters on the corner of James Street) and Cunard (with their home in one of the Three Graces). One other way to afford a bigger and more impressive building was to build an office larger than needed, and let out the extra space. The Royal Liver Insurance's Liver Building was a prominent example of this practice.

Lawyers' and accountants' offices could be found grouped around Cook Street, Harrington Street and North and South John Streets. These types of company often worked in an office block the company had built and paid for itself, as they often doubled up as estate agents. The focal point of this group of companies was the Law Association Building in Cook Street, whose door survives at No. 14.

Financial services had their centre on Castle Street from the nineteenth century. The Bank of England had opened a branch in the town in 1844 in a former private house on the corner with Cook Street, and this attracted other bank headquarters to the area. From then on all new bank headquarters located themselves on Castle Street. A related sector, and one with great importance to maritime Liverpool, was insurance, which clustered in Castle Street with the financiers along with

Different industries tended to congregate on the same streets in Liverpool, and in a similar matter so did the municipal functions. The Bridewell (below), fire station, education offices and council offices (right) all occupied sites around Dale Street, not far from the Town Hall.

MAIN   BRIDEWELL

some offices on Dale Street. The magnificent Royal Insurance Building on the corner of Dale Street and North John Street is one example, built in 1848 and replaced between 1896 and 1903. The Royal Liver Building, mentioned already, was one exception, preferring a prestigious Pier Head position.

Just as the industries of nineteenth-century Liverpool clustered in the same areas, the municipal functions of the town did too. Most of the Corporation's offices were in the Town Hall until the construction of the Municipal Buildings in 1868. When the move to the new buildings took place, it began a trend which saw similar council buildings located nearby, such as the magistrates' court, the Bridewell, on Cheapside, a fire station and education and tramway offices.

As politics and trade were so closely aligned, this clustering of offices allowed the convenient movement of the civic elite from one role to another. The two exceptions to this were the Customs House, which was located near the docklands and was the administrative centre for the port, and the offices of the Mersey Docks and Harbour Board, built on the filled-in George's Dock at the Pier Head. These buildings brought the administrative centre of gravity towards the river, but the separation from other municipal buildings caused problems due to their distance from similar functions.

Warehouses

When merchants lived next door to their warehouses this gave a degree of security for the goods stored. It was a simple arrangement as the goods were of such a type, and in such quantities, as to be easily kept this way. Some warehouses were built as tall and impressive wings to the merchants' houses, such as Thomas Parr's house on Colquitt Street. When trade increased in volume this became more difficult to do, and warehouses became separate buildings in their own right, or basements leased from office owners who wished to recoup some of the expense of building through rent. In addition, with merchants moving to the suburbs this option became much more convenient. So warehouses became separated from the owners' homes, and eventually also from the offices of the relevant company. The one exception to this was the food industry, whose rapid turnover of perishable goods meant that several town centre warehouses remained adjacent to the company offices.

As time went by, specialist jobs and eventually whole companies set up as 'warehouse keepers', such as the Liverpool Storage Co. Ltd and the Liverpool and Manchester Cotton and Produce Storage Co. Ltd. The earliest separate warehouses were built tall and narrow to make best use of the expensive land, and used hand-operated cranes to lift goods to the higher floors. For this reason you can still see former warehouses with a row of doors arranged vertically down one wall, each door allowing men inside to pull goods in from the crane, directly from the cart waiting on the road below. In one corner of the building was a steep stone staircase with a narrow door at the bottom and small

Warehouses were buildings designed with one function in mind, especially once merchants houses were no longer sited next door. Small windows and doors deterred thieves, and a vertical column of windows let in just enough light to illuminate the interior. In these former north docklands warehouses, shutters can be seen over tiny windows, and doors are small or reached by a narrow ladder to discourage theft.

grilled windows down its length. The small openings discouraged theft, as did the narrow stairwells.

After fires in the Goree warehouses on the Strand in 1802, and a number of other fires in 1842, local Building Acts were passed which made sure that floors and walls were of a minimum thickness. Building techniques, such as those used by Jesse Hartley in the Albert Dock, were developed to help prevent fire, or at least in the event of fire, to restrict it to as small an area as possible.

Offices

Companies with offices in Liverpool had to balance the need for a central location with its expense. One way of offsetting costs, as we have seen, was to rent out some of the floors to others who could not afford their own building. The offices themselves would usually be of three or four storeys, as this was a natural limit of the building technologies of the day. However, four-storey buildings were rare before the introduction of lifts, which made it easier to rent out the higher floors to others.

At the bottom of the building a semi-basement – a storey half underground which allowed a decent amount of light in – was usable either by the owners or their tenants, decreasing costs and improving efficiency. A further storey, a sub-basement, could be used as a lightless warehouse, which again could be used by the company which operated in the offices above, but more often than not was let out to a different one in need of town centre storage. Traces of these sub-basement warehouses can still be seen in the hoists which are present on the sides

In an effort to minimise the expense of a city centre office, many buildings included basements or semi-basements which could be used for storage or let out to others who could use the space. The half-hidden windows of basement shops today, and the presence of cranes on the side of buildings, reveals this former use, and the movement of goods into and out. Below this crane on Hackins Hey are the remains of an opening through which goods would be passed.

Built in 1864 and designed by Peter Ellis, Oriel Chambers was the first iron-framed building, a technology which enabled the skyscrapers of the next century. The great amount of glass used on its front elevation drew criticism, but was an innovative attempt to let in as much light as possible before electric lights were common. Natural light was important for the close inspection of cotton samples and other goods.

of buildings in the main city centre streets. Eventually this pattern of building took precedence over the previous warehouse/office/home hybrid.

The interior layout of an office was often of the dual type: an outer office for clerical workers at tall, sloping desks and a closed, rear office for the dealings of private business. In addition many would have a safe or a 'bookcase' (a strong room) for valuable records or money. For business partners, desks might be arranged opposite each other, and there might be an outer area where the public or customers might be met. The building itself would have to let in sufficient light for the inspection of samples, and so would have either large windows or a central skylight and stairwell. There was a move towards increased ornamentation in the nineteenth century, whereas in earlier years such decoration would have been seen as frivolous, and a sign of poor business acumen. However, practical considerations were still to the fore, and architects made every attempt to keep buildings bright without taking up excess space. Office rooms were arranged around a courtyard, with ceiling windows and white tiles making the most of the light which made it down into restricted building plots. Oriel Chambers, on Water Street, was the most startling example of these measures seen in its time, with 'bubbles' of glazing making up the front of the building, and extra detail added to the front elevation of a building which would previously have been kept plain and conservative.

THE PORT LANDSCAPE BEYOND THE DOCKS

By the start of the twentieth century the entire Liverpool waterfront consisted of docks and warehouses. One feature missing from this port was a shipbuilding presence. Shipyards were common in other ports, and had existed in Liverpool in the past, but the largest shipyard on the Mersey was on the opposite bank, at Cammell Laird in Birkenhead. The relegation of this seemingly central part of port life to another town demonstrates just how prized the waterfront was, and how focussed Liverpool's and the Corporation's use of land was at the height of its powers.

The biggest landscape influence on the shape of the Liverpool docks was the pressure from the built-up area of the city itself. Unlike port cities elsewhere, where docks were built on both sides of their river, Liverpool's docklands had to be built in a long strip of reclaimed land along the riverbank. Although this meant that new docks didn't have to compete with urban development when it came to find land, it did drag the docks away from the commercial hub – by 1900 the docks stretched over 9km from north to south, and this was even before the large developments at Gladstone and Seaforth docks.

Along the dock road, best seen today to the north along Regent Road, Jesse Hartley constructed a dock wall. In his 700th anniversary history of Liverpool, Ramsay Muir claimed it was 'as vast and enduring as the Pyramids, the most stupendous work of its kind that the will and power of man have ever created'.

The dock landscape of Liverpool extends beyond the basins themselves. The dock wall was a collossal anti-theft measure added by Jesse Hartley. This fronted onto the dock road, which separated the estate from the city. This caused some problems related to the movement of goods, creating congestion on the road and necessitating the creation of a rail station for almost every dock.

Even allowing for civic pride in the anniversary year, it is obvious that this structure was an imposing presence, declaring the might of Liverpool-as-port, also performing its more mundane job, that of deterring thieves. That theft was a problem demonstrates how open the docks were, and how free the access which contributed to the success of the docks as a transport and exchange hub.

The land on the other side of the dock road was given over to small-scale industry – flour mills, sugar refineries and warehouses — as well as other transport links taking goods beyond Merseyside such as the Leeds–Liverpool Canal and the railways. These transport hubs were the natural place for small businesses to cluster, being in a good position to support the general ebb and flow of shipping. In addition, each dock had become adapted for the type of cargo it most often dealt with, such as timber at Brunswick and corn at the Waterloos. This made it easier for dock workers and those in the supporting industries to locate themselves to best advantage.

Despite the carefully structured landscape of the docks, traffic flow was often a problem for the port. The Pier Head was a particular pinch point, with crowds of people milling around, perhaps to meet, promenade, or watch others coming from the ferries. This added to the general hustle and bustle of a busy area. But the town again adapted to the demands of commerce, and the rest of the commercial centre of the city moulded itself to best make use of the increasingly valuable land available (for example the filling in of George's Dock and its use for offices).

THE DECLINE OF THE TWENTIETH-CENTURY PORT

The twentieth century saw Liverpool's fortunes decline along with the British Empire. Imperial markets passing goods through Liverpool could still be relied on into the 1920s and '30s, but this was not to last. Soon after the First World War, in the shifting politics of early twentieth-century Britain and Europe, Liverpool was on the wrong side of the country. In addition, the 1929 Wall Street Crash and the Depression which followed caused serious problems on Merseyside.

A pivotal issue was Liverpool's total reliance on the proceeds of others' trade to survive. It was a transport hub, or it was nothing. The plans raised, then, were attempts to diversify the economy on Merseyside and ready it for the industries which would lead it boldly forward. Again the landscape played a part, and the large, open areas beyond the city boundaries were just the flexible blank slates the new century demanded for both its manufactories and its workforce.

Industry between the world wars

As Europe approached another war, measures were already being taken in Liverpool to shift its economy away from that of a trading hub to something more befitting a city of the twentieth century. The results of these measures were to drastically reshape the landscape around Merseyside.

The 1936 Liverpool Corporation Act allowed the city to build and lease out factories itself, in an effort to kick-start investment. One of the earliest fruits of the Act was the opening of Speke Industrial Estate, operating on 999-year leases and on which sixteen factories appeared by 1938. The Aintree Industrial Estate on Long Lane in Fazakerley was another new development area. It housed modern 'clean air' industries like food processing and electrical engineering, and

New industries moved in to take over the Royal Ordnance Factory sites after the end of the First World War. Areas like Aintree and Speke became new centres of industry. Some companies moved straight into old weapons factories, others like Bryant & May erected purpose-built factories in the same areas. The Match Factory, now reborn as the Matchworks, continues as an incubator for businesses in a part of Liverpool which has retained its industrial nature for nearly 100 years.

was conveniently located close to a labour force in the form of local residents in Fazakerley village. As war loomed, the distance of Liverpool's outskirts from Luftwaffe targets in the centre of town gave Aintree a degree of safety, resulting in the government locating Britain's Royal Ordnance Factories (ROFs) – ammunitions works – there in 1940, with a second ROF site out in Kirkby.

After the Second World War

During the Second World War, Liverpool experienced something of a temporary reprieve. Its central role in transatlantic food trade meant that it remained operational when other English ports were judged too dangerous to remain open. Despite the horrors of the Blitz, and the associated loss of life and buildings, Liverpool's economic good fortune continued into the next decades. With the end of the Second World War many in Liverpool found themselves in a period of post-austerity (relative) plenty. New industries came to Liverpool, occupying sites previously housing the Royal Ordnance Factories.

These factories shifted the area from military production to civilian work, and buildings such as aircraft engine works became rubber and electrical plants. The Merseyside Plan of 1944 continued moving people and companies out to the edge of town, creating thousands of jobs and housing the people who would fill them. However, much of these came at the expense of work in the city centre, and could not properly be considered to be 'new' jobs. Also, the decline in port activity was too swift for the new industries to take up the slack, and unemploy-

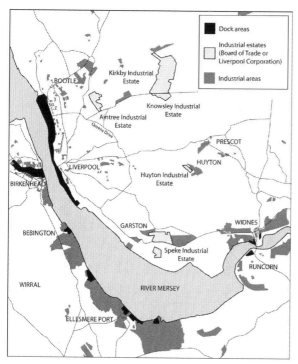

The new industrial estates which were built after the Second World War took advantage of buildings and infratructure used by the Royal Ordnance Factories (ROF). The land was flat and thus attractive to expanding companies. Along with the ready supply of labour soon to live in the council estates at Speke and Kirkby, these locations have remained centres of manufacturing ever since. (After Patmore, J.A. & Hodgkiss, A.G., *Merseyside in Maps*, p40, 1970, Longman)

ment figures were somewhat disappointing, despite the active role played by the MP for Huyton, Prime Minister Harold Wilson.

The port itself shifted its focus from textiles to metals and machinery in the 1960s. From these products it moved into consumer goods and high-tech industries such as vehicles. The port also dealt with bulk oil, with jetties at Tranmere and Dingle. However, there was a lot less diversity in Liverpool's cargo compared to the last century, and this left Liverpool at risk of changing tastes and demands. Alongside this the increasing containerisation of ports in general meant that the actual unpacking of goods (as opposed to the loading and unloading from ships) now took place far from the docks, often at the point of delivery.

In addition, Liverpool was adapting in many ways to an unfamiliar working environment. Independent-minded dock workers, used to the unpredictable fortunes of casual labour, found it hard to adapt to the monotony of assembly-line work, and some companies, notably Ford at Speke, discriminated against ex-dockers and sailors with a history of union activity. It must be said, however, that these new factories often embodied the modern world of large, well-ventilated places of work, with doctors and dentists offered as a service to workers. And as the austerity of the 1940s and '50s changed to an emerging wealth of the late '50s and '60s, Liverpool's fortunes appeared to be on the brink of a turnaround.

Resurgent wealth in 1950s–1960s

Once national and regional projects got underway to deal with the aftermath of the Second World War, a new age of optimism dawned. Not only were great plans made to reshape the city for the next century, but a new consumer boom shook off the austerity of wartime, and ships returned to the docks in great numbers. Dock workers and seamen were no longer casual labourers, and men came home from months at sea laden with gifts and wage packets which they seemed intent on spending before their next departure.

Liverpool became once more a transport hub for the country's industries – 44 per cent of workers in Liverpool were involved in the transport industry compared to 23 per cent nationally, while the rest of the country concentrated on manufacturing. Processing of raw materials was another Liverpool strength, with factories churning out tobacco (Ogden's), flour (at the Rank Flour Mills), sugar (Tate & Lyle remaining strong), biscuits (at Crawford's), sweets (such as Barker and Dobson's) and jam (Hartley's). The Bryant & May Matchworks near Speke used Baltic timber imported through the nearby Garston Docks as its raw material.

The South Docks were still used, although they were often too small for many modern ships and access from the river was difficult. The Albert Dock had gone out of use as a place to berth ships, but the warehouses remained in use well into the twentieth century. To combat the problems of an aging dock estate, £36 million investment was generated in order to modernise the Toxteth,

Harrington and Kings Docks, and to build a brand new dock at Seaforth which could adapt to changing trade technologies like shipping containers. However, Liverpool's narrow focus on only a few sectors left it vulnerable to changes in global patterns of change, and the decades which followed were to prove to be Liverpool's darkest.

Technological developments of the late twentieth century

Changes in passenger travel, and the rise of the airport, meant that people no longer needed to come to the Pier Head to board boats. This meant that city centre hotels and shops suffered from reduced trade at the same time as shipping lines lost their custom. The ultimate insult came in 1907 when the White Star Line moved its headquarters from Liverpool to Southampton, another symptom of the changing focus of travel and exchange. This drift to the south and south-east of England reflected a wider problem for Liverpool as Britain became much more a European country. The port was no longer in the unique position between the Old and New Worlds, between the raw material producers of Europe and their global markets. At the same time the standardisation of containers and ports meant that Liverpool no longer required its specialist dock workers – both dock staff and companies – in the move to mechanisation.

The two major continental ports were Rotterdam and Hamburg, with Felixstowe as the main port of entry to and from Britain. The Americas were no longer a major trade partner, so Liverpool, having for so long enjoyed great wealth from goods crossing the Atlantic, had to make do with serving the niche markets of Canada, Russia and some Mediterranean ports.

The docks continued to see a decline in use. In the second half of the twentieth century, the Manchester Ship Canal suddenly entered a period of success, bypassing Liverpool as goods were transported directly to its Lancashire neighbour. Although the tonnage going through Liverpool increased from a low in the 1980s of 50,000 TEU (20ft equivalent, based on a shipping container of that length) up to 600,000 TEU in 2004 (mostly timber grain and other bulk goods) much of the southern dock system remained too small to be of use. Their dereliction symbolised Liverpool's problems – investment had moved elsewhere, and no alternative use for them could be found.

The decline in work for Liverpool's docks had a knock-on effect for the existing problem of unemployment. An 11,000-ton container ship took 546 working hours to fully unload, compared to an ordinary ship's 10,584 hours. In 1967 11,500 people were employed on the docks, a number which fell to 5,200 in 1979. In the merchant navy, only half the number of crew were needed to maintain a container ship at sea, compared to a normal ship of similar size. This small crew would also carry out the maintenance of the ship in the shorter time that it spent being unloaded. This would normally have been done by a specialist dock company, while the ship's crew were in the port spending their wages. Therefore Liverpool's dockside cafes, pubs and shops were deprived of further income, as were the dock companies and those who supplied them, such as manufacturers of sacks, rope, boxes, paint and sack hooks.

Liverpool's days as a major city-port are over. The city will always be a port, but compared to its Victorian hey-day, it has diversified its industry, and its landscape reflects these changes. The shift in industry took place after the Second World War, as we have seen. But even in the previous century projects and institutions were being created which would have as much influence on the history of Merseyside as the new industries of the twentieth century. The philanthropic efforts of Liverpool's wealthiest men and women, as well as wide-ranging post-war urban plans, are some of the developments which have left the most visible traces in the modern landscape.

CHAPTER 6

RESHAPING THE CITY

Liverpool's efforts to improve its own physical landscape have a long history. Lord Street and North and South John Street were widened in 1826, when Liverpool was attempting to emulate the fashionable street architecture of London and Bath. Slum clearance attempted to improve the landscape, and was one of the earliest projects which changed the face of the inner city. Successors to the clearances carried on until the end of the twentieth century. This chapter looks at other nineteenth-century philanthropic and civic projects, from the laying out of Liverpool's largest parks to the establishment of institutional foundations – schools, church groups and training colleges.

During the Second World War the Blitz led to the loss of a great number of buildings as well as countless lives, and from 1945 the council took the opportunity for much more wide-ranging city centre rebuilding plans. These were intended to complement the slum clearance to generate a city fit for the future, but success varied. Whether or not they achieved their primary aims, however, these transformations have left us with the Liverpool of the twenty-first century, and the second half of the chapter looks at how they are still influencing the development of the city today.

PARKS AND GARDENS

The creation of parks and gardens was a response to two factors: concern for health, as already discussed, and the popular fashion of fresh air exercise. Parks were a way of helping deal with the living conditions of a rapidly expanding and overcrowded city. Ranelagh Gardens, which once lay where the Adelphi Hotel now stands, was an early example, but this was a private enterprise which charged an entrance fee, thus keeping it a rather exclusive location. In any case, Ranelagh Gardens closed in the 1790s, and Liverpool had very little open space to replace it. There were popular places like Everton Hill and Toxteth Park, which gave wide views over the town and its civic buildings, the River Mersey and beyond, but these areas were not set aside, and were used for small-scale industries like clothes drying, grazing and cloth tentering.

Residential squares were an early attempt to create a slice of nature in the urban area. Following similar developments in London and Edinburgh, George Square on Duke Street appeared in 1803 (with the popular Ladies Walk nearby),

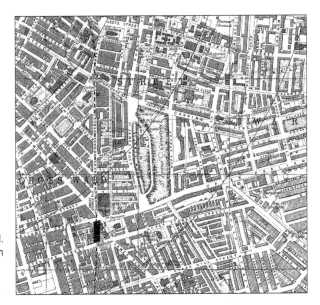

St James' Walk was one of the first parks in the town, following more specific entertainments like the Botanical and Zoological Gardens. It was laid out within the remains of a quarry from which much of the earliest stone buildings of the town would have been built. It was quite an exclusive location, situated in the new suburbs of the Mosslake Fields, but took security measures to ensure the park's genteel atmosphere was maintained. (Liverpool South Sheet, from *Plan of Liverpool 1890*)

Abercromby Square in 1815 and Falkner Square in 1835. These prestigious locations granted access only to residents, or those who purchased a key by subscription. These payments were well out of reach of most families in Liverpool, and so kept out the majority of the populace. The maintenance of the gardens was overseen by the Liverpool Corporate Garden Committee, who organised concerts, and residents were encouraged to report trespassers to the authorities to maintain the exclusivity of these spaces.

The first truly public open space was St James's Walk, on St James's Mount at the top of Brownlow Hill. Admission was free and the park had basic features, like a winding footpath, but very few structures. From the start it was treated by the Corporation as a more public space – comments were made that less attention had been given to the plantings here compared to the previous paid parks and the Faulkner and Abercromby Squares located not far away. However, the Corporation ensured the continuing quality of the park by prohibiting construction nearby which would spoil the view of the river, and smoking was banned in the 1840s. Grazing and market gardening were banned in any of the spaces in the town which were designated for leisure use.

In 1802 the Botanical Gardens opened on Myrtle Street, mixing leisure facilities with the growing public scientific interest. Access to the Gardens was again a restricted affair, requiring payment of a two guinea membership fee plus a letter of introduction. The Zoological Gardens was a related establishment. Though it charged only a shilling for a ticket, it still excluded the poorest in society, and therefore those with most need of open space.

Ultimately, however, the early parks like St James's Walk and the Botanical Gardens had a limited life. They were criticised for charging a fee, and being located in the wealthier parts of town. To make matters worse, as the dense urban fabric expanded to cover the hills around the town centre these wealthy residents moved away and the facilities became less used. The city encroached, with smoke from industrial processes deterring visitors even before such industries physically imposed upon the site, and the parks were not as popular with the wealthier citizens purely because there was no guarantee as to the 'quality' of the clientele. Security guards were already employed at St James Walk on Sundays, and later a policeman was stationed every evening from 3 p.m. until 9 p.m. to prevent damage by unwelcome intruders.

Truly public parks

It soon became clear that if the need for truly open space was to be met, then a full-scale civic project was needed. After such false starts as St James's Mount and the Botanical Gardens, Liverpool Corporation carried out a project to produce better parks. Princes Park was the first of these, laid out between 1842 and 1844 and named after the Prince of Wales. It was inspired by Regent's Park in London, and was the biggest project of its kind in Liverpool's history at the time.

Like Regent's Park, Princes Park consisted of a carefully constructed landscape surrounded by speculative housing. The hope was that the aspirational middle classes (those who couldn't afford to live further out of town) would buy up the houses, thus part-funding the park itself (see Chapter 4). The rest of the budget came from shareholders, and the land was bought at a cost of £50,000 from Lord Sefton. The design was by Joseph Paxton, a landscape gardener who had worked at the Chatsworth estate in Derbyshire, but was more famous for his designs for Birkenhead Park and the Crystal Palace in London.

Criticism came early as there was a closed-off area for the residents, and the highly ornamental nature of the park was judged unsuitable for general public use. Judged as part of wider efforts to improve public health, Princes was a failure. But aside from this the park was a popular attraction, and a Grand Fancy Fair was put on in 1849 to raise money for local hospitals. There was a huge number of stalls, demonstrations and even a balloon flight.

The criticism of Princes Park had not fallen on deaf ears, however. The Corporation now embarked on a much more ambitious park-building scheme, and in 1850 advertised a design competition. Only in 1865 did an Improvement Act allow the local government to raise the money to put the plans into action, but from 1868 to 1872 the parks of Stanley in north Liverpool, Newsham in the east and Sefton in the south began to take shape. The arrangement of the parks was deliberate: to provide a large open space for each area of the expanding town, by taking undeveloped land outside the city bounds and keeping it aside for leisure. For the first time the whole of the Liverpool public was truly kept in mind.

Newsham Park was to be laid out like Princes Park, with the cost to be met partly through the selling of large detached villas around its edge. Land was bought from Lord Molyneux, but plans were delayed by a period of economic instability in the middle of the nineteenth century. The winning design for Newsham was

As the decades moved on, more concerted efforts were made to create parks that the whole of society could enjoy. Princes Park was built for this purpose, although it didn't achieve this aim at first. However, it was the blueprint for later parks which were more successful, and was an important milestone in the development of facilities for recreation and fresh air. (Liverpool South Sheet, from *Plan of Liverpool 1890*)

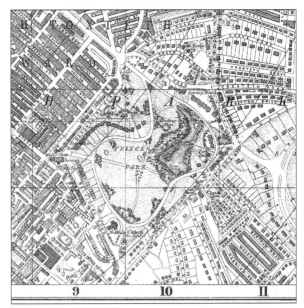

by Edward Kemp, previously a judge in the competition to design New York's Central Park, and consisted of three areas. The first was a wooded area with a boating pond; to the west of this was a large open area; and finally there was an undeveloped third area. Trees were planted and paths laid out to imitate a natural landscape, with the edge of the park cleverly hidden through coppices.

Raising money from auctioning off the land was more difficult than anticipated, and the addition of the Seaman's Orphanage in 1874 probably pushed prices down further. By the end of its construction cheaper alternatives had been used in order to keep within the budget, and many of the features were not as elaborate as they had been in the original plan.

Stanley Park, placed so as to serve the northern end of Liverpool, was planned in the 1860s. This was a time when Anfield was losing some of its wealth and exclusivity. Some big villas already stood in the area, but these had been built decades before, and so again the process of subsidising Stanley's building through the sale of speculative property was not as successful as hoped.

Stanley Park was a park of two halves: one was ornamental, while the other was for outdoor recreation such as football and cricket. The ornamental section, in addition to the flowerbeds which decorated the footpaths, had views over Anfield Cemetery and other open land which was still beyond the built-up area of Liverpool. There was also a key to show promenaders what they were looking at in the vista. This ornamental part was meant to fit with the 'wild' and natural areas to the north-east, and also contained the park's attractions like the aviary. The less decorative, more recreational areas of Stanley Park were designed with sports in mind, and were intended to complement the benefits of the rest of the park. This was hoped to be particularly beneficial to the working classes, and was where the earliest incarnation of Everton Football Club played their matches before moving to Anfield in 1884 (then Goodison Park in 1892).

Sefton Park was situated in the area inhabited by some of the wealthiest people in Liverpool at the time (and who had less need for Corporation-provided open spaces). It was planned with the inclusion of a private garden, and had more success in gaining funding through the sale of the villas surrounding it. The competition for Sefton's design was won by Edouard Andre, a former Jardinier Principal (head gardener) of Paris, and Lewis Hornblower, a local architect and designer of Birkenhead Park, and the entrance, lodges and gates of Princes Park. It was clear from the start that the expectations of the park's users was different to that of Stanley and Newsham. There were more ornamental features in Sefton than in the other parks, including drinking fountains, a boating lake, a grotto and an area for horse riding. Some of the features (such as Sefton Palm House and the Dell) demonstrated a commitment to continued long-term maintenance. The Palm House itself was donated by Henry Yates Thomson, who also donated a similar feature, the Gladstone Conservatory, to Stanley Park. The heating system, necessary for the tropical plants which were kept here, was constructed underground, beneath the glass houses themselves, to avoid cluttering the buildings' interiors or the surrounding park with bland maintenance structures.

The parks had originally been intended to ease the problems associated with the overcrowded and expanding town, but in practise they were more often the socialising spaces of the wealthy (particularly in the case of Sefton Park). Stanley Park was more successful in this sense, due to the emerging landscape of terraces and a less well-off community. Parks were also meant to be a safe haven from the dirt and squalor of the town. The gates were locked at night and patrolled by police or security guards. However, the parks soon gained a reputation for the night-time activities of those who managed to get around the security arrangements. They were also criticised for being built on land outside the town boundary, rather than on reclaimed land in the slums of the town centre. Because of their location they better served those who could already afford to travel to the open countryside, or even had a small slice of it in their own back gardens and grounds. However, in general the parks of Liverpool were a great improvement on the supply of green space for the Victorian city. They represent a huge investment in the quality of life of Liverpudlians by the Corporation, and set an example which other industrialised towns followed.

Parks in the twentieth century

With the construction of the parks in the previous century many Liverpudlians could enjoy walks, cycling or the handful of sports (football, cricket, bowls) catered for by the facilities. The parks attracted day-trippers from outside Liverpool too, such as (ironically) from the seaside resorts of New Brighton, Southport and Blackpool. Everyone would be entertained by regular events such as concerts, shows and the hot houses of Stanley and Sefton Parks. Children were particularly well catered for, with a children's garden in Stanley Park (based on *Alice's Adventures in Wonderland*) and both the Peter Pan statue and three pirate ships at Sefton. The Children's Festival in Stanley Park in 1904 was a prime example of the consideration given to youngsters. The idealism which produced these escapist areas for children was complimented by the sports activities, which were intended to encourage children to grow up strong and healthy – just the latest in a long string of measures to improve the health and wellbeing of Liverpudlians.

The parks changed over the years along with the fashions and needs of their users. Bowling greens and swimming pools were later insertions in the carefully planned landscapes. These facilities, along with the essential support buildings and changing rooms, were built in a variety of styles and materials, and could be seen to have damaged the carefully tended vistas of the Victorian parks. However, their flexibility in changing to suit the needs of their users was key to them maintaining their popularity into the new century.

Later on, more parks were opened, including Calderstones Park (1902), Otterspool Promenade (1950) and the International Garden Festival (albeit temporary, hosting the festival in 1984). Croxteth Park, the former grounds of Croxteth Hall, were given to the city in 1989 by the last Lady Sefton, and is still the largest public green space in the city. Netherley Park (1991-92), Fazakerley Ecology Park and the Liverpool Loop Line (a linear 'park' on the site of a former railway) are all integral parts of a continuing effort at urban regeneration, and are the latest generation of Liverpool's public green space projects.

The decline of the parks after the Second World War

The string of Victorian parks which encircled the city have survived in much the same form as originally laid out. However, they suffered somewhat from a lack of investment between the end of the Second World War and the close of the twentieth century.

The lasting effects of the First World War on the parks had been relatively minor. They had been used for military drills and practices, and some areas of them were used to grow food for the troops on the front. But little damage had been done and the landscapes recovered fairly quickly. The Second World War was a different matter. Iron railings which divided the different areas of the park were requisitioned for the war effort, and service buildings were destroyed by bombing.

Like many of the city's resources, public spaces were given over to the war effort in 1939. Sefton Park had barrage balloons (which stopped German planes flying too low while British fighters dealt with aircraft at higher altitudes), anti-aircraft (AA) guns and shelters for public use. Large areas were opened up to the 'Dig for Victory' campaign, both as collective fields and private allotments. This meant that much of the space was no longer usable for sports, although some was kept for this function for reasons of morale.

After the Second World War a lack of investment in the parks contributed to their further decay. Sefton Park was restored in 1953 but the railings in the rest of the park were not. The lack of railings had a longer-term effect, leaving parts of the park vulnerable to decay and vandalism. Statues which had been removed from the park for safekeeping were not returned. Funding followed policy away from the urban green spaces towards country parks on the edge of the city (such as Croxteth). A national trend was towards using less skilled workers to maintain the parks who, despite their enthusiasm, were not professional gardeners. There was no statutory duty for the council to maintain the parks, which were often treated as if they could maintain themselves.

In the late twentieth century Princes Park lost its Chinese Bridge and boat-houses to arson and other vandalism, and Dutch elm disease killed 700 trees in Sefton Park. However, in the closing decades of the century parks experienced a resurgence. Everton Park was laid out during the Militant Labour council's time in power in the early 1980s, as an integral part of their slum clearance scheme and, in the 1990s and 2000s, the hot houses at Sefton and Stanley Parks were restored with the help of community groups.

THE CORPORATION, MDHB AND CIVIC WORKS

The laying out of the parks around Liverpool's boundary was just one of a series of projects partly fuelled by a civic pride felt in local government, spurred on by local philanthropic sentiment. But there were concerns by the end of the eighteenth century that the line between civic philanthropy and the self-serving efforts of the rich in power was becoming blurred. It was certainly true that Liverpool's commercial interests and its political processes were both in the hands of a very select group of powerful and rich men. Over the centuries, the alder-men and councillors had gradually accrued privileges (such as the payments of rents, fines or customs) from the traditional power base, the nobility, and by 1800 it was generally the opinion that little benefit had found its way down the chain to the majority of citizens.

It is arguable whether improvement schemes such as the widening of Castle Street and the developments around Abercromby Square were for the wider town or simply those who lived and worked on those streets. This was even more of an issue as industry expanded in the town itself, and decreased the quality of life for those who could not afford to move out to developments such as Mosslake Fields.

The formation of the Mersey Docks and Harbour Board (MDHB) in 1858 brought some balance to the political power of the time. The members of the Board were mostly elected by users of the port of Liverpool, rather than mer-chants (who made up most of the council), while others were appointed by the national government, supporting those interests situated in Birkenhead and Liverpool's hinterland (see previous chapter). However, despite this, by the 1880s it was generally felt that the council, and not others such as the MDHB, were the best placed to manage the physical development of the town. This was particularly true once it became clear that the most generous philanthropists were members of the merchant elite, and therefore more likely to be on the council. Still, there were grumbles from the more mean-spirited councillors when taxes were used to fund the larger civic projects. Gradually philanthropy and civic spending became two accepted methods of furthering Liverpool's status through impressive building projects, town improvements and the fight against poverty and squalor. Donating money to civic projects became something of a competition, and it was debated whether the wealthiest were giving enough, or if the middling trades (building, food and drinks industries) were bearing a greater weight of generosity than the shipping merchants.

THE INSTITUTIONAL LANDSCAPE

The results of this philanthropy are still evident in the city today. Liverpool was growing at a massive rate as the nineteenth century progressed, producing the overcrowded slums in the centre of town, and increasing the movement of the richer classes out into the suburbs. We've already seen the Corporation's work to clear the slums, and provide extra green space for Liverpudlians, but in addition to this the town's wealthiest inhabitants (either out of a sense of guilt, religious compulsion or civic-humanitarian duty) donated money, buildings and other resources to develop institutions for the benefit of the vulnerable.

A burning social issue of the day – aside from disease, which affected every industrialised town in England – was the social problems brought about through Liverpool's nature as a port. Sailors were a particularly vulnerable element of society due to their transience in the town, and were often the victims of those who made a living separating them from their pay packets. Mariners also lived a dangerous life at sea, at great risk of dying and leaving behind their families, especially orphaned children. The Seaman's Hospital (part of the Infirmary on Shaw's Brow) opened in 1752, with the American Seaman's Hospital a related institution. The Sailors' Home, opened in 1844 and expanded on a new site in Canning Place in 1851, provided a place close to the docks for returning seaman to find a bed.

Other specialist institutions aimed to help further vulnerable sectors of the community, and put them to useful work. The Asylum for Indigent Blind was one such school, which first occupied two converted houses on Commutation Row before moving to a purpose-built building in 1800, demolished when Lime Street Station expanded. In 1851 the Asylum then moved to Hardman Street, where the building still stands, before expanding to the Royal Institute for the Blind in Wavertree. A workshop for the Outdoor Blind was built on Cornwallis Street in 1870, and its day visitors were put to work producing mats, brushes and baskets for sale. The Roman Catholic Blind Asylum on Yew Tree Lane in West Derby demonstrated a sectarian provision for the blind. It was set up in Islington in 1841 and relocated to West Derby (then on the city fringes) in 1899. The school had

A maritime theme ran through much of Liverpool's charitable organisations. The Sailor's Home probably remains one of the best known, and provided shelter and food for the many mariners who passed through the port. Mariners were vulnerable as men who spent only a little time in the town, and who could be conned out of their wage packet, or succumb to the many temptations of the port. (The Sailor's Home from the *Illustrated London News*, 1846)

its own farm supplying milk and vegetables. The Adult Deaf and Dumb Institute was established on Oxford Street in 1825, moving to its distinctive building on Princes Road later on. Other organisations set up to help children included the Blind Asylum, which had existed since 1791. It became the Blind School on London Road, and the children who attended weaved and sewed, making rugs, ropes, linen, sacking and fish lines, and were taught to play musical instruments.

The Mechanics Institute opened in 1825, initially for adults, but later it expanded to cater for boys as well. This philanthropic organisation, which was built to educate the children of the poorer classes, nevertheless had architecture which rivalled the wealthier organisations. Unlike some of the schools, the attendees were left to rely on their willpower to attend, drawing on their enthusiasm to bring themselves out of poverty through work.

Ragged Schools were smaller organisations, often set up by religious groups, who saw poverty and immorality in their own community and set out to do something about it. Father James Nugent, a Roman Catholic priest, and Canon Major Lester of St Mary's, Kirkdale, were prominent figures in this movement, setting up their schools to take care of the poor, and at the same time educate the younger generation in Christian morals and practical activities like tailoring, printing, and box making. This partly addressed the issue of 'street-arabs': young children who wandered the streets, sometimes becoming involved in petty crimes such as

The Institute for the Blind was an early institution which latterly occupied a building on Hardman Street, although was founded on Commutation Row in the eighteenth century. It provided training for the blind, and workshops for crafts, with day visitors making baskets, brushes and mats.

The Mechanics (now Liverpool) Institute was established to provide an education to all classes of society, and to encourage the poorest in society to work to pull themselves out of poverty. The Classical architectural style created a building which rivalled the splendour of the religious establishments in Liverpool and yet maintained its secular roots.

stealing 'swag' from the docks. Another of Nugent's projects, the Association of Providence, funded several schemes, such as the Boy's Night Shelter and Refuge in Soho Street, as well as orphanages, industrial schools and reformatories for those already involved in crime. The Ragged Schools were also seen as a front in the war on public houses, which sprang up on almost every street corner in the nineteenth century as the inner suburbs expanded. Targeting the young early was seen as a way to prevent a decline into immorality at a later date.

The West Derby Workhouse

The West Derby Workhouse, built on Brownlow Hill in around 1770, was a large and imposing building housing 5,000 inmates. It was a lesson – and a deterrent – for those who would fail in the Victorian system. Some of the most common people who entered the workhouse were the unemployed, who may have travelled to Liverpool seeking work. Others may simply have been unable to work, or struggling to take care of their dependents. Entrants were given a 'uniform' upon arrival, of easily identifiable clothes unsuitable for pawning. They were given a brief examination (including a check for repeat offenders) and washed. Those who were able were then given a couple of hours' work grinding corn in exchange for a bed and basic meal, before being sent on their way with three pence wages at the end of the day. In typical Victorian fashion, ladies of polite society were discouraged from entering the workhouse. However, Josephine Butler was one of those who did visit, and the workhouse became a key part in her tireless campaigning on behalf of vulnerable women in Liverpool.

Educational institutions

Education was another aspect of life which the city's influential citizens saw as key to dealing with social problems. Libraries offered a less formal educational resource than schools and institutes. The William Brown Library was very popular amongst the working class, but also favoured were the branch libraries set up in the inner suburbs specifically to offer local people the service, such as that in Athol Street just outside Kirkdale, and the Everton Library. Other libraries were built with a mixture of Corporate funding and philanthropic donation:

Local libraries represented the spread of education throughout the city. They were intended for use by those living locally, who would not travel to use a central facility. They were created through philanthropic donations (such as by Andrew Carnegie) and Corporation involvement. Several notable examples were designed by the Corporation Surveyor Thomas Shelmerdine.

the Kensington Library was the first of these, designed by architect Thomas Shelmerdine. Toxteth Library was another, opened by Andrew Carnegie in 1902 and also designed by Shelmerdine. Carnegie later offered £13,000 towards the opening of a second library in West Derby.

Education was seen as a way of raising working-class children out of poverty and giving them skills and instilling morals. Liverpool had had a grammar school since the earliest centuries of its existence, but this closed in 1810, and new schools opened to step into the gap. The Blue Coat School had been set up on School Lane in 1717 by Bryan Blundell for forty boys and ten girls. By 1824, 11,866 children were attending school at least once a week (including Sunday school), and further institutes were founded across the century to cater for all walks of life.

The Liverpool Academy of Arts in Seel Street was set up as a branch of the Royal Academy in London; schools such as the Anglican School in Everton Valley provided education with a religious slant, and the Collegiate on Shaw Street contained three schools (upper, middle and lower), with the lower specifically for those children destined for clerical jobs.

Religious and moral guidance

Religious groups were as active as individual citizens in working to provide moral teaching and practical skills to those in their community. In 1886 the Gordon Working Lads Institute was opened in Kirkdale by ship-owner William Cliff in memory of his son. Metalworking and woodworking classes, plumbing, arithmetic and writing classes were all designed to benefit those children who might otherwise be on the street. Three years later Bernard Hall, a merchant, opened the Florence Institute in Toxteth to educate boys in Christianity and the Bible, although free of specific sectarian interests. The same year Bankhall Girls Institute on Stanley Road was funded by Thomas Worthington Cookson with similar aims for girls.

All these schools included sports activities and drill training, and had their own brass bands. There was a focus on discipline and self-respect, and many were sited close to public houses. The pubs were often built in showy coloured bricks and glazed tiling, in an attempt to entice drinkers. The schools set themselves up as moral guides, and as a direct alternative to a life spent in a bar room. The schools buildings copied the techniques of the public houses, either through distinctive building materials or awe-inspiring architecture. The Florence Institute was built from orange brick, with a tall corner tower (once holding an onion dome on top). The fittings inside the buildings were also designed to impress, and it was hoped the children who enjoyed the finely decorated room would be therefore encouraged to aspire to success.

Baths and wash houses

City-funded medical services were a more direct approach to dealing with the specific problem of disease. The wash houses were the earliest and perhaps least formal of these, but can be seen as the evolution of even older buildings. The Corporation had built George's Dock baths in 1828 when Liverpool still aspired to be a spa town. Later, public baths were also built in Westminster Road, Kirkdale in 1876, and Beacon Street, close to the docks and poor housing. The earliest baths were more of a leisure facility than a medical one, but equating cleanliness with health was already cemented in the minds of Liverpudlians. However, the baths lacked facilities for properly washing linen, one of the best tools in the fight against disease.

When an outbreak of cholera struck in 1832, Kitty Wilkinson, a working-class Irish immigrant, set up her cellar as a wash house for use by her neighbours. This was principally for washing clothes which had come into contact with a victim of cholera. Elizabeth Rathbone, part of the famous philanthropic dynasty, helped Wilkinson expand her efforts, until the Corporation took notice and set up the first public wash house in Upper Frederick Street in 1842, with Wilkinson appointed supervisor. At the wash house was a room for washing infected clothes, which was free to use with a note from the Medical Officer. In later wash houses the room for washing clothing was completely separate from the rest of the facility, further helping prevent the spread of disease.

Hospitals

The wash houses had been adopted by Elizabeth Rathbone, but a more formal civic establishment was the Infirmary. Built in 1749 on the corner of Shaw's Brow and Lime Street, the Infirmary expanded twice in the late nineteenth century; moving to Brownlow Hill in 1824 when demand outstripped facilities. In 1890 it was rebuilt to the designs of Alfred Waterhouse (designer of other Liverpool buildings, such as the Victoria Building of the university) in Pembroke Place, acquiring a central location from which to serve the whole town.

Apart from the main Infirmary, a range of specialist hospitals appeared which together constituted Liverpool's medical provision. The David Lewis Northern (1834) and the Royal Southern (1842) hospitals were built closer to the docks, and somewhat eased the demand on the Infirmary. The School of Tropical Medicine, also on Pembroke Place, was an obvious advantage to a port with extensive contacts across the world, and was part-funded by Alfred Jones, a merchant with particular interests in West African trade. The Stanley Hospital was built on Stanley Street, Kirkdale, in 1867, and enlarged in 1874 after a short period of closure. The Lunatic Asylum was built in the gardens of the original Infirmary in 1792, when it was located on Shaw's Brow. A dispensary for the distribution of medicines was also located on Shaw's Brow from the late eighteenth century, with a second on Great Mersey Street in Kirkdale. By the end of the nineteenth century there were three hospitals, four dispensaries and over twenty other specialist institutions for specific ailments.

The Brownlow Hill Infirmiary was a major addition to the institutional landscape when this building was opened in 1890. Designed by Alfred Waterhouse, it was used until 1978, and lay empty until bought back by Liverpool University in 1994 for use as part of clinical training. (Robert Cutts, Creative Commons Attribution 2.0 Generic (CC BY 2.0))

THE LANDSCAPE OF BROWNLOW HILL

Brownlow Hill is something of a special case in the institutional landscape of Liverpool. By the start of the twentieth century a great number of hospitals, educational establishments and social provisions had accumulated in this small area of town. A hundred years previously this had been open fields, and like the Mosslake Fields nearby it was first developed as a wealthy residential suburb. However, a series of new organisations grew up in the area over the course of the nineteenth century, which resulted in the concentration of institutional buildings we can see in the landscape today. The first was the workhouse between Brownlow Hill and Mount Pleasant in 1771, but others followed. As the area developed into an institutional area the wealthy residents moved out. This in turn freed up high-quality buildings to be occupied by new schools and charities, and so the process fed itself over the course of a hundred years.

The area also proved useful to the University of Liverpool. While it was a part of the federal Manchester-based Victoria University, University College Liverpool moved from its initial location, in a disused lunatic asylum, into the purpose-built Victoria Building. Designed by Alfred Waterhouse, the location situated the university in the same district as other Liverpool institutions, and inevitably gave rise to a growing number other buildings in the area being adopted by departments and administration offices. Thus today the university buildings occupy an area intermingled with the landscape of nineteenth-century civic institutions.

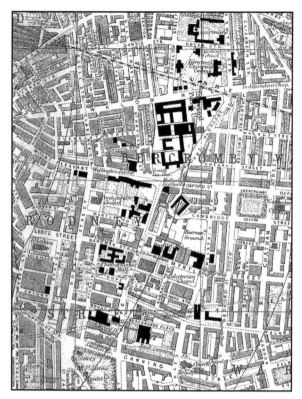

The workhouse was one of the first institutional buildings to occupy a space in Mosslake Fields, but soon others joined it until the area was populated by a range of similar charitable organisations. Now the area from the Metropolitan Cathedral to the Angican is dotted with current or former buildings concerned with works to help the poor, sick or vulnerable in society, creating an 'institutional landscape' within the city, indicated on this map by the solid black buildings. (After Giles, C., *Building a Better Society: Liverpool's historic institutional buildings*, 2008, Fig. 74)

In 1938 the three general hospitals (the Infirmary and the Northern and Southern) came together under the name Royal Liverpool United Hospitals. It was decided that a combined, city-centre site was needed to help serve the whole of Liverpool, and so another of Waterhouse's masterpieces, the Royal Infirmary on Pembroke Place, added another major resident to the Brownlow Hill landscape. Then, in 1978, post-war redevelopment required the building of a modern and larger hospital for Liverpool, and the Royal Liverpool University Hospital building opened on Prescot Street.

The Brownlow Hill landscape was completed over the course of the twentieth century, with the addition of two cathedrals. The Anglican Cathedral was the first to be begun, soon after Liverpool was granted a bishopric in 1880. An architectural competition was won by Giles Gilbert Scott, but a site had to be decided on. Various locations were put forward, starting with St John's church behind St George's Hall, followed by St Peter's and St Luke's churches and the triangle of London Road and Pembroke Place. All were found to be too small for the scale imagined for the cathedral, and so the fifth option, the open space of St James Mount, was chosen, placing the future cathedral at the southern end of the Brownlow Hill Group.

The choice of location for the Catholic Metropolitan Cathedral was of similar convenience. The Local Government Act of 1929 gave cities permission to take over workhouses following a Royal Commission report of 1905, which had found that such institutions were unsuited for dealing with the huge variety of cases they were given. More specific organisations were recommended, and so the life of the general deterrent workhouses had come to an end. This freed up a large space for the construction of a new cathedral. Still working to the original Edwin Lutyens design, the workhouse was demolished in 1931 and construction began. Despite the massive alteration in the design following post-war austerity, the cathedral today still inhabits the location of the workhouse, completing the institutional landscape unintentionally begun by its predecessor on the site.

WILLIAM BROWN STREET/ST GEORGE'S PLATEAU

St George's Plateau and Lime Street constitute another special case demonstrating the effect on landscape that Liverpool's philanthropic and civic works could have. The area became the prime example of what could be achieved with a mixture of civic pride, vast corporate wealth, and a will to improve the quality of life and the town environment. Lime Street Station was the earliest of the large buildings in the area, having been built in 1836 as the terminus of the Liverpool-Manchester Railway. For the first time Liverpool had the station it deserved, bringing passengers right into the town centre itself (rather than being brought in from Edge Hill by carriage, as had been the case beforehand). It also created

The area around Lime Street has long been a gateway into the city, where the roads from Prescot and London enter the town itself. Following the construction of several major cultural buildings on William Brown Street, plus St George's Hall and Lime Street Station in the nineteenth century, the area became a gallery of civic pride, showcasing transport, justice, fine entertainments and artistic culture in close proximity. Any visitor alighting a train or carriage would be in no doubt as to Liverpool's attempt to position itself as a major player on the Victorian stage.

William Brown Street (formerly Shaw's Brow) became a cultural centre with the gradual accumulation of a museum, gallery, library and law courts. This row of buildings was created with a combination of civic and philanthropic funds, of which the greatest came from William Brown himself, who donated funds for the museum which at one point bore his name.

a perfect spot in which to place Liverpool's finest architectural gems, and the opportunity was not missed.

St George's Hall itself was the result of two competitions held to design a concert and assize court. When a young Harvey Lonsdale Elmes won both he was asked to combine them into one structure. The foundation stone was laid in 1838, on the former site of the Infirmary, with construction work lasting from 1842 until 1854. Sadly, Elmes died at the age of thirty-four in 1847, never living to see his masterpiece completed. The project was carried on by the architect C.R. Cockerell, who also designed the lavish interior of the hall. St John's church, which until this time had sat on the land to the west, was removed to make way for St John's Gardens, which became another of the fashionable promenades which existed across the town.

From this beginning Shaw's Brow, running down one side of St John's Gardens, attracted more impressive architecture beginning with the William Brown Library in 1860. Its intended purpose was to house the natural history collection of the thirteenth Earl of Derby, which the earl had bequeathed to the town in 1851. The original museum, the Derby Museum on Duke Street, had outgrown its original building, and the William Brown Library and Museum (still the building's official name today) became its new purpose-built home. William Brown himself sold the land for the museum, and funded much of its construction, and so the road was renamed from Shaw's Brow to William Brown Street in his honour.

The Picton Reading Room was the next building to be begun on the street, to designs by Cornelius Sherlock modelled on the reading room of the British Library. It took its name from James Picton, architect of many of Liverpool's finest buildings and the author of one of the major histories of the town. By the time the Picton Reading Room was completed in 1879, the Walker Art Gallery had joined the group, having been completed in 1877 and designed by H.H.Vale. The statue above the entrance depicts Liverpool personified, with a trident in one hand to represent the sea, and a propeller in the other to represent the shipping and trade which was so central to Liverpool's success (and its ability to afford such prestigious building projects as these). The Sessions House, built in 1884, was designed by F. and G. Holme, and completed the strip of imposing Victorian cultural institutions.

The Steble Fountain, which sits at the top of William Brown Street, was presented to the town in 1879 by Colonel R.F. Steble, a former mayor. The Wellington Memorial which sits alongside was designed by George Anderson Lawton of Glasgow. The statue of the victorious duke was cast from the metal of captured French guns. Trade was still not far from the mind here, shown by the display of iron pegs on the west side which mark out a standard measurement table of the Board of Trade.

And so by the end of the nineteenth century the centre of Liverpool had a spectacular collection of fine architecture right on its doorstep. Visitors to Liverpool would arrive at the town either via rail at Lime Street Station, or carriage via London Road, entering the town centre facing William Brown Street. Either entrance would be in the shadow of the imposing St George's Hall, a demonstration of culture, justice and architectural taste, not to mention power and money. William Brown Street would show off Liverpool citizens' historical and cultural wealth and education, and the grand entrance to Lime Street Station would remind the visitor of Liverpool's position at the forefront of transport technologies. If a visitor had any lingering doubts as to Liverpool's position as Second City of Empire, or as Britain's pre-eminent port, then this panorama would be swift to dispel them.

URBAN RENEWAL IN THE TWENTIETH CENTURY

The Second World War had a devastating effect on Liverpool's urban landscape. Vast swathes of the city centre were flattened by the Luftwaffe, the pressure on the existing housing stock increased, and the city faced an unprecedented need to reconstruct whole areas of land. We have seen the many projects in housing which were initiated by the post-war City Council, which moved huge numbers of people out of the centre into edge-of-town housing estates, but there were also grand plans for the centre.

In response to city-centre bomb damage, wide-ranging City Plans were drawn up in 1942 (even before the war had ended) and 1953, while The Merseyside Plan 1944 had been published before the war was even over. However, other priori-

After the widespread damage caused during the Second World War, plans were drawn up to rebuild. Houses needed replacing, and new estates were planned, but the centre of town was the subject of much more holistic views for a 'city of the future'. Two of these plans, created by Shennan and Shankland, envisioned grand schemes affecting the whole of the city centre, but social and economic factors meant that nothing like this saw the light of day. (Liverpool Record Office, Liverpool Libraries)

ties (addressing the congested road system, housing shortages and clearing bomb sites) meant that it was only in 1959 that implementation of the plans began.

Graeme Shankland had been appointed city planner in 1961, with the hope that his expertise in complete urban renewal (in Milton Keynes, London's East End, and several American cities) would rise to the unique challenge Liverpool faced. Shankland's vision was for a 'bold, ambitious, design-led plan for a major city', and included 7.5 million square feet of new office space on Old Hall Street, Moorfields, Lime Street and near Central Station. Shopping arcades were planned in the form of St John's Precinct, Clayton Square, Central Station, Paradise Street and the Strand. In addition to offices and shops there were to be civic amenities such as central parks and a civic arcade.

Transportation needs were to be taken care of by a 'loop and link' underground railway between the three central stations (notably those areas targeted by new office developments) and a separation of vehicles and pedestrians through the construction of raised walkways giving access to buildings on higher floors. Motor traffic would be completely removed from the main shopping streets. The new tunnel to Wallasey would take some of the strain from the Queensway tunnel (see Chapter 7), connecting a proposed mid-Wirral motorway to the centre of Liverpool and an intended eight-lane inner elevated ring road. Scotland Road was to be completely remodelled to accommodate the approach to the tunnel. While the major City Plans were never completed in their entirety, the new Kingsway Tunnel, a handful of raised road and walkways and significant changes

The changes made to the centre of Liverpool in the 1960s and 1970s was unprecendented, with large scale projects intigated to bring the city into the modern era, and to deal with the increasing problem of traffic. A long stretch of Scotland Road was demolished and remodelled, sweeping away communities and housing, and making way for the entrance to the second Mersey Tunnel, the Kingsway. (Liverpool Record Office, Liverpool Libraries)

to the shopping district around St John's Market were eventually built.

These first two decades after the Second World War saw a return to the Mersey of much of the shipping lost in the inter-war years. The city regained its sense of optimism, buoyed by an increase in wealth and the prospects of new industries out in Speke, Kirkby and Aintree (see Chapter 5). Even when Liverpool found itself on the wane again in the second half of the twentieth century, plans were drawn up to counter the increasing pull of London and the south. At its most futuristic and ambitious this involved a supercity, or 'city of the future', a proposed 'Lancaston' stretching across the county with Liverpool as its port. More realistic, yet no less ambitious, plans included massive council housing estates and whole New Towns, with Kirkby, Skelmersdale, Winsford and Cantril Farm being the largest. City-centre plans were no less radical, and potentially no less damaging. Kenneth Thomson, MP for Toxteth, supported a fourteen-lane ring road through the town centre. Fortunately for the coherence of the town centre, widespread and growing public opposition saw it scrapped as an idea.

Unfortunately, such optimism did not last far into the second half of the century. New economic problems dogged Liverpool, and many of the road and housing schemes ran out of funding. Much of the Modernist schemes of raised

Part of the modernist plans to reshape the centre involved new concepts such as raised walkways, to separate pedestrians from motor vehicles. These were never popular, and proved expensive, and so only a handful were ever constructed. However, traces of the scheme can still be seen on office blocks in the business district of the town centre, where first-floor balconies around Old Hall Street and Tithebarn Street were originally intended to give access from the walkways straight into the offices.

walkways and high-rise living became unpopular realities, attracting vandalism and eventually exhibiting the poor quality of the materials used. Today many offices to the north of the city centre retain evidence of the planned first-storey walkways, and pay testament to the unfinished nature of many of the dreams of the new planners.

Late twentieth-century urban regeneration

A new era began in the 1970s with the formation of the Merseyside County Council (MCC) in 1976. The Merseyside Development Corporation (MDC) took over plans for urban renewal from Liverpool City Council and drew up a new scheme for the South Docks. However, the economy was weak, and the new Thatcher government of 1979 would give no financial support to help buy the docks. Instead, it instigated the 1980 Local Government Planning and Land Act which established the Urban Development Corporations (UDC) to encourage the reclamation of derelict land and in turn private development. The Merseyside UDC was established in 1981, with a remit covering 350 hectares of the South Docks, parts of the Sefton North Docks and land on the Wirral. It was with the creation of this body that the Albert Dock scheme got underway (previously abandoned as an idea by the City Council), with the initial aim simply to dredge the contaminated silt from the docks and restore water to them, in the hope that this would initiate private investment. That the whole of the central dock area is now a thriving shopping and tourism centre, complete with high-profile destinations like the Tate and the Merseyside Maritime and International Slavery Museums, attests to the eventual success of the project. This was a flagship scheme for Merseyside, at the forefront of an era of redevelopment which would stretch across the town centre and beyond.

Following the Toxteth riots and a national realisation that there were some severe problems in Liverpool, Michael Heseltine was appointed 'Minister for Merseyside', and the Merseyside Task Force (MTF) was set up in 1983. Like its predecessors, the MTF hoped to spark new private sector investment and development, and Wavertree Technology Park (on the site of disused railway sidings) was one of the first successes. However, Liverpool was about to move more heavily into heritage and tourism, as the MTF's schemes had more success in this sector as well as the service sector.

Whereas the MDC had had little success by this point, the MTF charged them with creating the International Garden Festival. The festival took less than two and a half years to bring to fruition, reclaimed derelict and contaminated land next to the river, and reviews of the event (as well as the wider reclamation project as a whole) were very positive. Although there were problems in trying to find a permanent solution for the use of the land once the fesival ended, the Landscape Institute named it as the Most Infuential Landscape Scheme, 1970–2002, due to its wide appeal and lasting legacy.

By the closing years of the 1980s Liverpool had two successful transformations under its belt, in the shape of the Albert Dock and the Garden Festival. Both these projects gave the city the confidence to move towards a strategy which

The Albert Dock played another pioneering role in the late twentieth century, being a flagship regeneration project at the heart of the city. Many projects were put forward as solutions to the abandoned warehouses, but in the end the docks became a mixture of shops, museums, a gallery and television studios. The basin was dredged and water returned to it, and the scheme became a model for the regeneration of Liverpool's disused historic buildings.

One of the more recent developments, Liverpool One is the latest structure to occupy the site of the Old Dock, following in the footsteps of the Customs House and Chevasse Park, the latter now incorporated into the shopping centre. Liverpool One helps bridge the former gap between the business and shopping centre around Lord Street and the dock developments on the riverside. Heritage is at the heart of the development, with historic tide measurements incorporated into the fountains, or old warehouses transformed into modern retail units.

involved tourism rather than the traditional areas of manufacturing and transport. More renewal plans in the 1990s were brought together under the banner of the Single Regeneration Budget (SRB). Whereas the council had been some-what sidelined under the Urban Development Corporation model, the regional office of English Partnerships encouraged it to become more closely involved in regeneration, with a range of private, public and voluntary groups in partnership. The Liverpool Institute of Performing Arts (LIPA) and Blackburne House were at the hub of regeneration of the Hope Street area, and benefited from the city's successful bid for City Challenge money in 1992. Ironically, the poor economic conditions of the last three decades of the twentieth century aided regenera-tion, as large areas of fine Georgian and Victorian heritage survived (albeit after a period of neglect) to be brought back into use for various university functions and some private housing.

Recent developments and the future of Liverpool

In later decades new schemes were created to make up for the mistakes of the old ones. Cantril Farm had become infamous, but was redesigned as Stockbridge Village, a partnership housing scheme set in motion after Michael Heseltine's visit in 1981. Clayton Square was redeveloped into a modern shopping centre, although debate still runs as to whether this was an improvement on the original Georgian cityscape. The civic buildings clustered around St George's plateau were cleaned in the 1980s, the better to display to visitors the architectural achievements of what was once the second city of Empire.

Redevelopment continued into the twenty-first century, with wide-reaching projects to redevelop the location of the Old Dock into the Liverpool One shopping centre and Canning Street into a major thoroughfare. As we go into the second decade of the twenty-first century, the company which owns much of Liverpool's dock estate, Peel Holdings, has proposed a massive redevelopment scheme for the North Docks, which have long remained disused. The plans have drawn criticism from the government's historic adviser, English Heritage, as well as from some local campaign groups, but it remains to be seen whether, given planning permission, this becomes one of the defining developments of the Liverpool landscape's next 100 years.

CHAPTER 7

ROADS,RAILS,TUNNELSANDTRACKS

At the centre of a global network of trade routes, Liverpool's success depended greatly on transport. But if the docks were the gateways of this network, other transport links were the keys which gave passage through them. Canals, and later railways, were used to move goods to Manchester and other parts of the hinterland, and improvements to these internal links were essential if Liverpool was to keep up with its competitors. The extension and development of the transport network – including completely new modes of transport like motorways and airports – constrained and shaped Liverpool's landscape and its future in equal measure.

THE RAILWAYS

The Liverpool of the nineteenth century, situated on the west coast of England, was finding a role for itself as a trading and transport hub. It sat on the border between the north and south of England, between the Midlands and the North Wales coast, and between Europe and the New World. While its transatlantic routes were strong and growing in the nineteenth century, its links to and from the manufacturing centres and markets of south Lancashire and Yorkshire relied on the Mersey & Irwell Navigation and the Bridgewater Canal. Both these channels were from another age; they were slow and unreliable, drying up in summer and prone to winter freezing. They were also held by strong lordly and business interests, and were expensive. It was often joked that goods took longer to get from Liverpool to Manchester than they had taken to cross the Atlantic, and indeed cargoes could sit in Liverpool warehouses for weeks awaiting transportation further into Britain.

Even before the building of the first intercity rail route between Manchester and Liverpool, Merseyside was familiar with steam-drawn trains. Jesse Hartley's dock rail system used both horse-drawn and mechanical trains in its time. The problems of this pioneering network were that the rails and the buildings that came with them competed for land with docks and warehouses near the river front, and there was little space for the decent-sized sidings or marshalling yards that a successful system required. Goods had to be stored in dock warehouses instead of rail goods sheds, and so by the time the system was complete there was almost one station per dock. This was inefficient, caused congestion and wasted time, and meant that the main line of the railway was separated from the dock-land estate itself by the dock road.

It was becoming clear by the 1820s that if Liverpool was to continue its growth, a better and faster link with nearby towns and cities was needed, and the infrastructure in the city itself needed to be reconsidered. Calls were made by local businessmen for the Dock Trustees to address the issue, and Acts of Parliament were sought for the permissions needed to carry out such a huge project. However, the first decision which needed to be made was: should a new railway use stationary or locomotive steam engines?

Rainhill Trials

The Rainhill Trials were an essential engineering step in the introduction of rail, and in the construction of the new Liverpool to Manchester line. But they were also a spectacle. A course was laid out in front of grandstands for spectators, the track representing the 70 or so miles that trains would have to run between the cities. On the day of the trials a brass band, bunting and a huge crowd only added to the excitement.

The competition rules had been very exacting, and demanding of the technologies of the time. Engines had to consume their own smoke, and pull 20 tons at 20 mph. The vehicles themselves should be spring-mounted, and no more than 60 tons (due to caution over travelling across the unsteady Chat Moss bog). They needed to operate with a boiler pressure of no more than 50lbs per square inch (psi), and have safety valves and a steam gauge. Most importantly of all, they had to be ready for the trial on 1 October 1829.

In the event there were five competitors, including one optimistic entry involving a horse attached to a treadmill. The engines competed to varying success, but suffice to say that George Stephenson's Rocket was the only one which came well within its weight limit, not even pushing itself to capacity. In fact, it was the only locomotive which completed the course, and earned Stephenson the £500 prize and a contract to produce the engines for the Liverpool and Manchester Railway.

The Liverpool-Manchester Railway

In order to get the necessary parliamentary permissions for the new railway, an accurate survey of the route needed to be submitted. Two were carried out, the first by George Stephenson and then a second by George Rennie, Stephenson's having been thrown out of Parliament for inaccuracies. The first Bill for the new railway had been put through Parliament in 1825, four years before the Rainhill Trials, and had been defeated at the committee stage by a single vote. Two major objectors to the project were the earls of Derby and Sefton, through whose rural estates this noisy, dirty machine would pass. Unsurprisingly, those who held financial interest in the canals also argued against this competitor. However, eventually the project got underway, with the construction of embankments, the excavation of cuttings through the solid Liverpool sandstone, and the building of such engineering feats as the Sankey

Viaduct and a 'floating' raft to carry the rails over Chat Moss. The gas-lit Wapping Tunnel was dug from Edge Hill Station (the terminus for passengers) through to Wapping Station near Wapping Dock, with the names of the roads above painted on the whitewashed walls. Further, the Olive Mount cutting between Edge Hill and the city boundary required a 70ft by 20ft stretch of solid rock to be blasted out.

The opening day of the Liverpool-Manchester Railway on 15 September 1830 was a memorable one, if partly for the wrong reasons. Crowds lined the route from Crown Street, Liverpool, to Liverpool Road, Manchester, taking up vantage points on the new embankments and bridges along the way. The trials of the day have been recounted by historians enough to times to be familiar. William Huskisson MP was tragically killed during a short stop. The reception in Manchester for the Prime Minister (the Duke of Wellington), so soon after the Peterloo Massacre, was beset with rioting and other disturbances. The duke never left the train, making an unscheduled and chaotic journey back to Liverpool, to arrive at 10 p.m. that night. Despite these inauspicious beginnings, however, the railway was open, and set to change the landscape of Liverpool and the rest of the world in a very short time.

Route and stations

The new railway had some of the longest-lasting impacts on the Liverpool landscape, some of which can still be seen today. The route began from Wapping Station (later known as Park Street Goods Station) near the docks, travelling through the Wapping Tunnel to Edge Hill via Crown Street Station. This was the first tunnel built under a city, opening with the railway in 1830. The remains of the tunnel can still be seen at the Wapping end, although the station itself was demolished soon after it closed in 1972. The other end of the tunnel is also open to the air, if not the casual tourist, as one of three arches near Edge Hill Station.

At the opening of the railway, Crown Street – around half a mile west of Edge Hill – was the Liverpool passenger terminus. The steep incline from Edge Hill meant carriages coming from Manchester had to be detached from the locomotive at Edge Hill Station and pulled the rest of the way by a stationary steam engine attached to a rope system. By this method the train would ascend through a single track tunnel to Crown Street, while goods trains would then descend through the 1.25-mile Wapping Tunnel to the docks. The mechanism for the rope hauling engine was housed in the Moorish Arch which stood near to Edge Hill Station on Cavendish Drive. When Lime Street Station opened in 1836 as a more useful and central terminus, Crown Street Station closed, but in the early years the journey from Edge Hill to the new terminus was still done by brakeman-controlled descent, returning via the rope-hauled mechanism.

From Edge Hill trains made their way to Liverpool Road, Manchester via Broad Green (still the oldest working railway station in the world), Roby, Huyton Hay and Huyton Quarry. Cargo could use the Canada Dock Branch which ran north through Walton to the docks, while other trains used the Cheshire Lines Committee's line heading towards Allerton in the south.

Liverpool was a pioneer in rail travel, and its early routes changed several times in their first decades. Remnants of these old routes are still to be seen, such as the Wapping Tunnel ventilation building on Blackburne Place (left) and the entrance to the Wapping Tunnel at Kings Dock Street.

Railways in Liverpool

The opening of the Liverpool-Manchester Railway was the beginning of a transport revolution across the world, and the town of Liverpool was to be transformed by the new infrastructure needed. Lime Street Station had opened in 1836, and more new stations opened regularly to carry passengers right into the centre, rather than have them alight at Crown Street and travel the rest of the way by carriage. More new stations opened regularly over the next decades, with Exchange Station opening in 1850 and Central in 1874. Exchange Station expanded in 1886 to deal with the increasing volume of traffic, and the Mersey Rail Tunnel of 1886 soon became an alternative to crossing the river by ferry. By 1900, 9 per cent of land in central Liverpool was owned by railway companies, including the dock railways and the Overhead Railway.

Nevertheless, the railways brought some problems to the town at the same time. They aggravated the problem of overcrowding as railway companies bought large parcels of land for tracks and, especially, stations. They bought the cheapest land, clearing it of the slums that stood there before but without building any housing elsewhere to replace it. In addition the layout of the docks meant that railways couldn't run alongside; each dock therefore had to have its own goods terminal. But in spite of these problems the trains quickly became a popular and familiar part of the landscape, and helped Liverpool's growth from the time of their inception.

Suburban railways

The biggest factor in rail's favour was that it opened up commuting to a new wave of workers. Suddenly, more of Liverpool's numerous clerks and middle office workers could afford to travel further to work, and might even be able to afford a house further out in the suburbs, such as in Anfield or Tuebrook. The Cheshire Line Committee's North Liverpool Extension Line (NLEL, opened 1879-80, now the Liverpool Loop Line cycle route) served a string of suburbs from Halewood to Walton Triangle junction, splitting off from there to Aintree (serving race-goers), Kirkdale and the docks. Its success meant that in 1884 it was extended from Aintree to Southport, riding on the back of an increase in tourist travel to the seaside resort.

A second Cheshire Lines Committee (CLC) route ran from the southern suburbs of Garston, Chessington and Aigburth, promoting the growth of southern Liverpool. The line ended at Garston Station, and in the beginning travellers heading for the town centre had to alight here and go the rest of the way on a Cheshire Lines-provided horse-drawn carriage, which dropped passengers at their headquarters in James Street. This situation was somewhat improved in 1874 by the opening of Central Station by the CLC. Brunswick Station, another out-of-town passenger terminus (of the Garston and Liverpool railway) closed in the same year, from then on handling only goods.

In the 1920s new large residential estates were served by stations opening in Clubmoor and Warbreck. The Mersey Railway which connected

Until the middle of the twentieth century Merseyside had a comprehensive network of local railway routes, bringing passengers from across the country as well as transporting them around Liverpool. Many of these were reduced to solely goods routes as the passenger services became less popular, and many subsequently closed. Today, the routes may have been redeveloped into cycle routes, with the stations (such as West Derby, shown) still visible along the way.

Liverpool to the Wirral (see below) created a second network operating on the western side of town, but the opening of the underground loop in central Liverpool in 1972 allowed a greater co-ordination between the disparate lines, and joined the routes into a Merseyside-wide rail network. In the following three decades new stations on existing routes brought technology parks (such as Wavertree) into the network, and in 2006 Liverpool South Parkway effectively connected the rail and bus network with Liverpool's John Lennon Airport. Many of the places these lines served around the outskirts of Liverpool were villages before the railway arrived. These villages were all eventually swallowed up the expanding city, and the railways must be seen as a factor in this development.

The NLEL began to decline after the Second World War. Childwall Station was always slightly isolated from the small village it served, and had closed to passengers in 1931, then to goods in 1943. In 1952 the Southport service closed, and in 1960 the line from Aintree to Gateacre became a victim of Beeching's axe, closing to passengers. From this date on the majority of rolling stock carried goods to Huskisson Dock and the north riverfront area. Also in 1960 the Aintree Central and Manchester services were withdrawn. The Gateacre to Liverpool Central trains carried on until 1972, if only to help with the building of the underground central loop railway in that year. The last goods train ran in 1975, and, over the course of a few weeks in 1979, a demolition train removed the tracks. The route lay abandoned for some years, until the southern extent became part of the Halewood Triangle Country Park and the rest was tarmacked and became a well-used cycle route.

The Liverpool Overhead Railway

By the closing decades of the nineteenth century Liverpool had an extensive dock estate, stretching 9km from north to south along the river. This created a narrow channel down which all dock traffic had to flow, in comparison with other port cities where the docks formed a hub around which the city could operate. This meant that traffic on the dock road was a dangerous mixture of pedestrians and heavy goods vehicles, and becoming an increasing problem. Jesse Hartley's horse-drawn trains on the dock road were often a source of the congestion, and often had to leave the tracks in order to get around obstructions like cargo being dumped in the middle of the road.

The ship-owners were some of the people most inconvenienced by this state of affairs, and so it is little surprise that Alfred Holt, founder of the Blue Funnel cargo steamship line, was the first to ask the Mersey Docks and Harbour Board to take action in 1877. His proposal was for an overhead tramway for passengers, which would leave the dock road free for goods traffic. Hartley was initially opposed to the idea as it would get in the way of his plans for further new docks and so make them more expensive.

Nevertheless, Acts were passed in 1878 and 1882 giving permission to construct an overhead railway, though nothing happened on the ground. Meanwhile, across the Atlantic, New York built a raised railway in 1881. Finally, in 1888 the Liverpool Overhead Railway Company was formed to take on the construction task. The company was allowed to make compulsory purchases of land in exchange for passing on a share of their profits to the MDHB. Incidentally, the MDHB saw this as an opportunity to buy land for its own improvements at a better-than-market rate.

An early decision was made to use electric engines rather than steam as there was a worry that sparks from steam engines would present a fire hazard to the flammable cargoes they passed by. For a railway that was to be suspended on tracks above the road the lighter electric locomotives held an advantage over their steam-driven counterparts. Electric vehicles were also more flexible, allowing them to navigate the many twists and turns that a journey along the dock road would involve. Thus, taking their inspiration from American successes with electric, a formal decision was made to construct an electrically driven raised railway along the dock road, along with the necessary power station to supply it. Further Acts of Parliament defined the route from Alexandra Dock in the north to Herculaneum in the south. £450,000 was raised, part-funded by the MDHB, and J. W. Willans of Manchester was contracted to build it.

Building the LOR

Dock road congestion meant there was very little space to construct the railway. Therefore it was prebuilt in sections elsewhere before being assembled on-site. The tracks were to be placed at a height of 50ft above the road, with individual spans between 30 and 70ft long. The winding route, however, meant that few of these 'standard' spans could be used, and many had to be made to measure.

There had been a proposal to lean the raised platform against Hartley's colossal dock wall, but it was found that even this was not strong enough. The solution adopted was to build a free-standing structure. Specially built gantries moved along the constructed sections, lifting new spans into place before moving on to the next. It was then a simple job of laying tracks on the completed lengths. One concern for the designers was the potential for things to fall from the tracks onto the road below, causing hazards. For this reason the surface of the viaduct on which track ran was completely sealed and waterproofed (creating the 'docker's umbrella').

The route

The Overhead Railway was opened by Lord Salisbury on 6 March 1893. It was immediately popular with dockworkers and general passengers, particularly when the line was extended beyond the docks to Seaforth in 1894 and the Dingle in 1896. By this date, there were fifteen stations on the line, with the trains taking a little over half an hour to go from one end to the other.

The railway quickly grew beyond a mere dock workers' commuting route,

STRAND STREET AND OVERHEAD RAILWAY, LIVERPOOL   19083

The Liverpool Overhead Railway ran along the dock road in an effort to reduce congestion. It was raised above the roadway to avoid causing as many problems as it solved, and could carry passengers the length of the docks in little over half an hour. Here it passes the Three Graces and the Pier Head station. (From a postcard by J. Salmon)

becoming a tourist attraction in its own right. Since the building of the great dock wall it had become impossible to view the inner workings of the estate, but now anyone with a ticket had an almost bird's-eye view of the whole complex. And even though Liverpool had lost its waterfront promenades and bathing facilities to industry and commerce, the LOR attracted those who wished to visit the city's civic centre, or as one stage in a journey across the Mersey to New Brighton. At its peak in 1919 over 19 million passengers used the route in a year.

The end of the LOR

Of course, technologies change, and competition in the form of the new electric trams (see below) hit the LOR hard. Trams had lower fares, and with the concessions granted to them by their owners (the Corporation) they would always have the natural advantage. The telephone, another technological innovation, made obsolete the messenger boys used for communication between the docks. The economic difficulties of the inter-war period further reduced passenger numbers, just as maintenance costs were increasing. It had initially been calculated that 9 million passengers were needed per year to make the railway viable, but this figure was revised upwards from the 1930s to the 1950s while no money was set aside for repairs and maintenance. The iron from which the LOR was built was vulnerable to corrosion, and the money for repairs simply did not exist. Finally, extensive bomb damage during the Blitz put the rebuilding of the LOR out of reach of the city, and the LOR closed on 30 December 1956. Over the course

Parts of the Overhead Railway still exist, having been left in place when the rest of the structure was dismantled. Some uprights are visible next to the dock road north of the city centre, and the entrance to the Dingle tunnel is easy to spot in the south docklands.

of the next year the infrastructure for the railway was demolished and removed, with a few uprights and the entrance to the Dingle tunnel being the only surviving features left to mark its presence.

THE MERSEY RAIL TUNNEL

As with many of Liverpool's new transport links, the Mersey Tunnel was a means of improving the overburdened routes which existed at the start of the Victorian period. The ferries were the sole means of getting across to the Wirral, but even before the wide introduction of motorised road cargo transport the ferries were under strain. A road tunnel had been proposed as early as 1825, but the expense of constructing such a thing, and difficulties relating to building exits in densely packed areas of inner-city Liverpool meant that the project was never realised. An early idea for a bridge had fallen foul of the same problems. One of the more serious initial plans was for a pneumatic (air-driven) tunnel, and indeed such a project was granted an Act of Parliament. This would have worked around the problem of smoky steam trains travelling through the confined space under the river, but the available technology of the day was not up to the task, and this idea was abandoned.

In 1871, another Act of Parliament gave permission for a rail tunnel to be built under the Mersey, but it was not until 1879 that one Major Samuel Isaac began actual excavation of a trial tunnel. Isaac's trial was a success, and the tunnel proper was soon begun, hand-excavated with picks and explosives until replaced with a new machine, the Beaumont Cutter. The speed of the excavation thereafter increased rapidly, continuing day and night, and the tunnels from either bank met in January 1884. Two years later the structure was complete, and was opened by the Prince of Wales on 20 January 1886, with pedestrians permitted to walk through the tunnel before the first trains began to run.

The new Mersey Rail Tunnel was 26ft (8m) by 19ft (6m) and in addition to the main two-track tunnel two further channels were made, for ventilation and drainage respectively, with pumping houses at ground level to move air and water out. The tunnel was also used to carry telephone cables from Liverpool to the Wirral.

The stations linked were James Street in Liverpool and Hamilton Square in Birkenhead. So deep did the stations need to be that lifts were required to take passengers down to the platform level; hydraulic (water-powered) lifts suitable for a hundred passengers were installed at both locations. The knock-on effect of this was the construction of huge five-storey towers at both stations to house the lift mechanism and water storage. The tower at Hamilton Street survives to this day, but its partner at James Street was destroyed in the Blitz of 1941.

The tunnel was immediately popular, with 2.5 million people using it in the first six months, and 10 million annually in later years. It was more reliable than the ferries, which could be affected by the weather, and offered a 15-minute journey across the river. However, success did not last long. In 1887 the Mersey Railway Company went bankrupt. The initial enthusiasm of the public had waned due to the poor atmosphere underground. The specially adapted engines which were meant to contain and collect all their own steam did not work effectively. The hugely expensive ventilation pumps did not work efficiently either, making the problem worse. The development of the tram network meant that there were excellent connections between the tram termini on either side of the Mersey, linked by a hop on the ferries.

Despite this period of bankruptcy, however, the Mersey Railway Company survived, and made efforts to improve their service. The railway was extended to Rock Ferry in 1891 and to Chester in 1895, and on the Liverpool side extensions ran from James Street to Central Station's then-new Low Level platform in 1892.

From 1900 the old steam engines were replaced by electrically powered vehi-

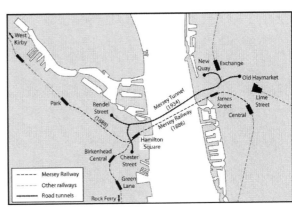

The Mersey Rail Tunnel was built as part of the network joining each bank of the river. Built in 1886 and electrified in 1903, it joined Liverpool's Central Station with Birkenhead and stops beyond. Little apart from electrification changed until a loop was added in central Liverpool in the 1970s. (After Patmore, J.A. & Hodgkiss, A.G., *Merseyside in Maps*, p52, 1970, Longman)

To carry passengers down from street level to
the underground platform, hydraulic lifts were
incorporated into the stations at Hamilton
Square and James Street. The lifts were large –
carrying 100 commuters – and so the hydraulics
required huge towers to hold the water needed.
That on James Street was detroyed during the
Blitz, but Hamilton Square retains its own, a stark
reminder of the technology once used to operate
it. (J. Speakman)

cles which helped to reduce the poor
air problem. New tracks were laid and
the network rejuvenated, the switcho-
ver taking place overnight on 2 May
1903. These efforts paid off and helped
to restore the number of passengers on
the network. The building of the cross-
river tunnel and the extensions from
the city centre to other central stations
helped create a cross-Merseyside rail
network.

The story of the railway in Liverpool began with a pioneering project to connect two cities. It drew a straight, industrial line through the patchwork of fields
in south Lancashire, marking the landscape forever. This new technology was an
immediate success, and soon a web of interconnected lines helped open up the
outskirts of Liverpool to new development. Despite the closures of many lines in
the middle of the last century, Liverpool still boasts the busiest commuter rail network outside London, a direct legacy of those Victorian efforts. Routes like the
Overhead Railway and the Rail Tunnel completed the network, helping power
Liverpool through the Industrial Revolution, and leaving a legacy of architectural
remains which still tell the story of the beginnings of rail.

ROADS ACROSS MERSEYSIDE

Roads are ubiquitous features in the landscape, perhaps the greatest measure of
urbanisation available to the landscape historian. A study of the roads in a city
can map expansion, wealth, population and even health when other research is
factored in. Liverpool's Victorian expansion can be seen laid out in the change
in road patterns from the inner city outwards to the suburbs, in the redeveloped
thoroughfares of Scotland Road and Great George Street, and the ultra-modern
developments of flyovers and motorways.

By the beginning of the twentieth century much of central Liverpool's map
was already drawn: the original seven streets were still present in the middle of
the town, the roads leading out from the centre were those main thoroughfares

which had carried carts and traders into the hinterland and beyond. But networks of new streets were being built, with the expansion of the existing suburbs and the opening up of new ones. Even today it's possible to identify and contrast the regular gridiron patterns of the Victorian streets in Everton, Walton, Wavertree, Kirkdale, Anfield and Kensington with the later curving roads and boulevards of Norris Green, Dovecote and Allerton. The long, straight streets dotted with large houses in West Derby and Anfield were gradually replaced with regular grids of semi-detached 1930s housing and Victorian terraces respectively. Parts of south Liverpool have both these types of housing in close proximity. Housing of the 1950s tends to appear on similarly regular roads as the 1930s, seen in parts of Walton amongst other places.

The 1960s modernist high-rise buildings which replaced the Victorian slums were in turn demolished in the 1980s. The sites on which they sat are now parklands in Everton, sitting alongside truncated roads which were once part of the vast grid of now-lost Victorian terraces. Areas of clearances are given away by the presence of blocked through-routes and modern housing amidst old churches and terraces. A family historian might come across an ancestor's road only to find it filled with twentieth-century bungalows.

Other groups of roads imitate those of earlier periods. Some found in West Derby, Walton and Mossley Hill have similar grid-like arrangements to the Victorian suburbs, but are more widely spaced and contain the larger semi-detached housing of the 1930s. Housing from near the end of the twentieth century, on large estates on the edge of the city such as Croxteth Park, try to

The housing in Everton was replaced with tower blocks (one group, consisting of Crosbie, Canterbury and Haigh Heights, were known colloquially as the Piggeries) and so a large amount of open space was created and turned into an urban park.

As well as the remains of former streets, older buildings such as churches survive in the modern landscape. In addition, old walls may tell of former land use, having been incorporated into new developments. Here, Cochrane Street, which once ran from Heyworth Street to Netherfield Road, has been reduced to a shadow of its former self. Only the church now remains, surrounded by car parking where once terraces stood.

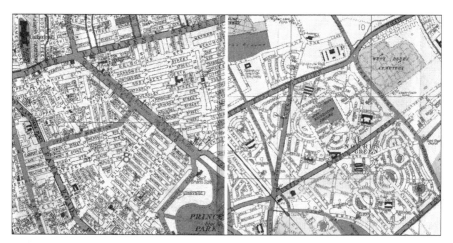

The arrangement of streets in an area, as seen on the map, can tell us a lot about the age of the houses. The Victorian pattern was of a gridiron of tightly packed streets, whereas interwar housing was often built on geometrically curving roads. More modern housing estates tried to emulate the curving (but not geometrical) patterns of old village centres, although close inspection reveals hidden regularities in the engineered curves. (Extracts from *Geographia Plan of Liverpool and Bootle, c.*1950)

imitate the winding irregular streets of ancient village centres.

Village centres

A noteworthy feature of the roads of Liverpool, and seen on any map, is the preservation of old village centres in street patterns and road names. Villages which were once separate from Liverpool but were eventually swallowed up stand out from the surrounding areas due to the more irregular shape of the roads, or the distinctive and often older architecture you can see on the ground. Particularly obvious centres are those of Everton, Bootle, Walton and West Derby. A careful look at a map shows a small knot of streets representing the original village centre. Gateacre centre is fairly easy to recognise when passing through, with the village green, fountain and older architecture contrasting with the post-war housing which grew up when the area became a suburb in the 1950s and '60s.

Winding its way through the middle of all these developments is Queens Drive, Liverpool's Ring Road. Queens Drive is perhaps the most succinct case study of Liverpool's forward-thinking engineering, the vision of the city engineer J.A. Brodie. A ring road was something long proposed for Liverpool, particularly when it began to grow in earnest in the second half of the nineteenth century. When the scheme was finally considered seriously, three ring roads were planned, but only Queens Drive, the central one, was built. The ring road concept tied in with the ribbon of parks (see Chapter 6) which was another of the great civic projects of that time.

Begun in 1904, the earliest sections of the road were at the north end, from Rice Lane to Larkhill. By 1910 the road stretched to Mossley Hill via Broadgreen and Childwall. As it went, Queens Drive took in existing roads, widening them

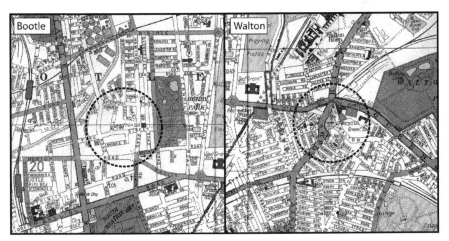

The ancient village centres have, more often than not, been preserved even as Liverpool engulfed them. The less regular shapes reveal these centres, as do the road names in some cases. In some instances all the buildings have changed, but the village shape can be traced in successive maps. (Extracts from *Geographia Plan of Liverpool and Bootle*, c.1950)

or straightening them, sometimes bridging gaps across empty fields. The ultimate aim was to link up with Aigburth Road in the south of the city, which would in turn take visitors back into the city centre. This never happened, and instead the dual carriageway section of Queens Drive now stops at Mossley Hill, before continuing as two lanes down to Sefton Park, where it stops at the junction with Mossley Hill Drive.

Even without considering the great engineering undertaking that Queens Drive represents, what is most startling is the vast swathe of green space it drove through when first opened. Photographs of the time show the bare earth of the first excavations bordered either side with loose picket fences and miles of rural countryside. That Liverpool was expanding at an exponential rate was not in doubt even then, but Brodie's forethought of the importance of linking all present and future parts of the city (and, more to the point, his recognition of the increasing importance of car travel) should not be underestimated.

The new highway, that opened up areas for residential development, had knock-on effects in the widening of radial roads such as Prescot Road and West Derby Road, and prompted the construction of new ones such as Walton Hall Avenue and Edge Lane Drive. It remains a defining feature of the map, an outline of the Victorian city and a monument to one of its defining figures.

Brodie had been visionary in his plans for a large ring road, even before the areas it served had been developed. After the Second World War, Liverpool's city leaders found themselves responsible for a city where cars were becoming ever more common, and industry ever more greedy for transport. The 1949 Lancashire Roads Plan was drawn up in response to this perceived need, and identified Liverpool as a hub of trade, serving the important areas of Lancashire

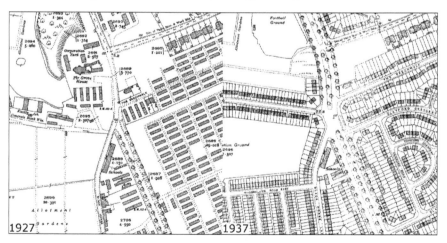

The designing and laying out of Queens Drive was a large project, and one which showed the foresight of its engineer J.A. Brodie. Stretches of the Drive took in older roads where possible, transforming them into a road suitable for turning into a dual carriageway decades before cars became ubiquitous. (Ordnance Survey map of Lancashire and Furness, 1927 (left) and 1937 (right), 1:2500)

and Yorkshire. Later came the 1962 Mersey Traffic Survey, which aimed to take a more carefully measured census of traffic, in light of new centres of industry in the form of the Ford factory at one end of the city and the new and intended docks at the other. One of the results of this was that the City Surveyor proposed an Outer Ring Road to help deal with the traffic, and it was out of this proposal that Liverpool's motorway network was born.

Motorways

From the 1960s Liverpool became newly connected to the rest of the country via a number of new motorways. The M62 was intended to link Liverpool and Hull – the great northern ports – to the manufacturing districts of Yorkshire and Lancashire. This was a colossal project, costing the best part of a billion pounds in today's money, but the Liverpool end is a slightly odd arrangement which reveals that the original plans did not see the light of day. When construction began the M62 (originally labelled the M52) should have taken drivers onto the proposed Liverpool Inner Motorway (LIM), and right up the the Kingsway Tunnel (see below) and on to the Wirral and Cheshire. However, as the LIM was never built, the link wasn't either, and today the M62 comes to a premature halt at Junction 4, on Queens Drive at Broadgreen.

The ring road proposed by the Mersey Traffic Survey in 1962 appeared in the form of the M57. It was completed in two phases from 1972-74, and was a direct response to the perceived need for improvements in road transport supplying the northern docks, including the brand new container dock at Seaforth. Like Queens Drive, the M57 linked up the radial roads leading into the centre of town, and was initially intended to circumnavigate the city of Liverpool from Crosby to Halewood. However, like its sister the M62, it was never completed to plan, though it is a reminder of the projects which tried to attract and maintain industry in the troubled years of the middle to late twentieth century.

The M58 was intended as a link between Liverpool and the M6, taking in the New Town of Skelmersdale along the way. It opened in 1968 with a single carriageway in each direction, but was gradually upgraded with more lanes, reaching official 'motorway' status in 1977. Much of its length was constructed on an embankment, with the ground built up in places using black shale from coal pits in the St Helens area.

ROAD TUNNELS

The Mersey's famous ferries had provided cross-river transport for centuries, but the growth of cargo road vehicles in the twentieth century threatened to bring Liverpool to a standstill. Queues of trucks and lorries waiting for the ferries caused gridlock even in the first two decades of the century, and so a plan was needed to ease the pressure on the boats. A rail tunnel had existed since 1886, and the first proposal for a road tunnel came sixty years before that. However, it was only in the 1920s that the need for such a project outweighed all objections and delays, and in 1925 the first ground was broken for a Liverpool to Birkenhead road tunnel, to be known as Queensway.

Passengers were well served by the combination of ferries and the rail tunnel, and so the prime concern was for (mainly commercial) vehicle crossings. Because of this a bridge was proposed between Liverpool and Birkenhead, but such a plan was judged untenable. Apart from the cost, a bridge might block the river, or be a target in time of war. The footings of the bridge could also cause the river to silt up, creating problems for shipping and increasing the costs of dredging to keep the river clear. And so the tunnel was settled on, and granted through an Act of Parliament, with the government to fund half, the Liverpool and Birkenhead ratepayers a quarter, and the remainder from tolls on the tunnel users. The costs of maintenance would be borne by the ratepayers.

Great effort went into the construction of the Queensway Tunnel, and the architect H.J. Rowse was appointed to create the entranceway ornamentation. His distinctive style (he also designed the Martin's Bank building and the Philharmonic Hall) was applied to the frieze above the entrance, and the design for the ventilation tower – properly known as George's Dock Ventilation and Control Station – which still operates from behind the Three Graces at the Pier Head. (Gene Hunt, Creative Commons Attribution 2.0 Generic (CC BY 2.0))

The excavating machines were begun by Princess Mary, Viscountess Lascelles, with a golden key in December 1925, and the two pilot tunnels dug from the banks met in 1928, ceremoniously broken through by Margaret Beavan, Lord Mayor of Liverpool, and Alec Naylor, Mayor of Birkenhead. Although the tunnel was bored through the bedrock along the underwater stretch, those parts on the riverbanks were excavated using a cut-and-cover technique. So, for example, a stretch of Dale Street was excavated before having a cover placed over the top of it. King George IV opened the tunnel on 18 July 1934.

The landscape of the tunnels

The now familiar parts of the tunnel landscape, as it shows itself in Liverpool, were not those originally intended. The Liverpool entrance was originally intended for Whitechapel, before Old Haymarket was decided on, and the Birkenhead entrance was moved twice.

On the Liverpool side, land was purchased and the buildings cleared from an area to the north-east of Old Haymarket. On this site the Queensway Tunnel entrance was built: a road sloping down into the darkness surrounded by Herbert J. Rowse's modernist decoration. Rowse designed the archway and its parapet (with space for statues of King George and Queen Mary), as well as the toll booths and the lighting columns which graced either end (of which only the Birkenhead one survives).

Moving further down to the Pier Head, another of Rowse's architectural masterpieces is the George's Dock Building, sitting behind the Port of Liverpool building. This draws fresh air into the tunnels, extracts the exhaust gasses of the vehicles, and doubles as the offices of the Mersey Tunnels division of Merseytravel who administer the tunnel's operation.

Around 1.2 million tonnes of rock, gravel and clay were removed to dig the tunnel, much of which was used to build another of Liverpool's well-known landmarks, Otterspool Promenade. When it was opened in 1934 it was the longest underwater tunnel in the world at over 2 miles long. The tunnel itself was built with a circular cross-section, with the road deck as a separate structure hanging half way down. This means that there is a large space beneath the road, and original plans were to run an electric tram here, and later a gas mains. Neither of these projects came to fruition, however, and now the space is used as part of the ventilation system and for cable services.

As well as the main channel, Queensway has two branch tunnels, one on either side of the river. These were designed to serve the two dock estates on the banks of the Mersey, again to help separate traffic of different types and so ease congestion. With the building of the Kingsway Tunnel in the 1960s the Birkenhead branch was closed, but the entrance is still visible on Rendell Street, complete with Rowse architecture. The branch on the Liverpool side remains open, letting vehicles out onto The Strand at the bottom of Chapel Street.

The Kingsway Tunnel

By the 1960s several changes had been made to deal with the increasing traffic. The Queensway itself had been a response to higher levels of cargo on the roads, alongside commuters and holidaymakers, and adjustments had been made to that scheme during and after its opening to deal with higher car ownership, longer commutes and even greater numbers of goods vehicles. The flyovers around the Queensway entrance and William Brown Street were an attempt to separate traffic heading for the city centre from that wanting to cross the river. A similar scheme on the Wirral shores has only recently been removed.

But soon all these measures would prove insufficient, and by 1947 there was such a great number of tunnel users that tolls were paying for all maintenance without the need for ratepayers' contributions. A grander scheme was needed to deal with the traffic. Consultants recommended a six-lane bridge to cross the Mersey, but the cost of this, plus the inability to decide on the best route, meant that once again a tunnel was in the offing, first proposed in 1958.

An Act of Parliament in 1965 authorised the construction of the second Mersey road tunnel, Kingsway, at a cost of £7.5 million. Typical of the more ambitious construction schemes of the decade, the Kingsway entrance sits within a labyrinth of flyovers and raised roads. There was anger at the number of houses demolished to make way for the link between the tunnel entrance and Scotland Road, which had also been greatly redeveloped in this period. This more modern tunnel entrance (opened by Queen Elizabeth II in 1971) had a much greater impact on the landscape, on both sides of the river, than the one constructed thirty years previously.

No less striking are the ventilation shafts of Kingsway. Standing sentinel over the Mersey on both sides are these gigantic concrete and brick buildings. Two intakes sit either side of a central chimney, the whole design – Sharples called it 'imposingly sculptural' – looking for a balance between functionality and appearance. The locations of the newer vents – industrial docklands rather than the

The Kingsway ventilation building is no less distinctive than the Queensway, though it is in a very different style. Twinned with another across the Mersey, the shaft is located in a more industrial area than its older counterpart, and built in a style Joseph Sharples compared to 'a rocket on its launchpad'.

central commercial area – seems typical of a more modern approach to separating moving traffic from busy centres.

The two tunnels were built in response to rising vehicle traffic. The first road tunnel was an engineering marvel of its day, and drew on several well-known personalities in its construction, including H.J. Rowse and J.A. Brodie. The second tunnel, Kingsway, was a much larger, industrial-scale project, carried out to deal with the unprecedented popularity of the motor in the second half of the century. Both schemes contributed to a 'shrinking' of Merseyside, for improved transport links ease movement across greater distances.

OMNIBUSES AND TRAMS

For a city to expand, it is not enough simply to increase the size and number of roads. When population density in Liverpool was predicted to become a serious problem at the turn of the twentieth century one of the solutions was to encourage and enable people to move away from the centre. Visionaries like J.A. Brodie foresaw that a network of affordable tram routes was a way to achieve this. With the increasing wealth of the middle classes (clerks and middle professionals), more people could afford to commute, and the tram system serviced this need well.

The first scheme approximating a tramway was a 'street railway' which operated along the Dock Road in 1859. Two years later a short length of horse-drawn tram was opened as the Old Swan Tramway, but it's likely that this consisted of a single car, and the business closed in under a year. The first hint at a proper system was a section of test track laid in Castle Street in 1865 by the Liverpool Tramway Company (LTC). Although the track was eventually abandoned, the system had proven itself and in 1868 an Act of Parliament gave the LTC permission for an Inner Circle route and lines to Walton and Dingle.

The project was completed quickly, with the first tram leaving its shed in the same year (1869) as the first tracks were laid. There were sixteen cars in all on this new network, with three horses each, and 7,000 passengers were served on the first day alone. The trams were successful immediately, and by 1875 over 60 miles had been laid across the city, with 207 cars and 2,894 horses at work.

The network faced difficulties in the decades which followed. Ownership changed hands several times: a merger between the Liverpool Road and Railway Omnibus Company and the LTC in 1876 was followed three years later with the purchase, by the Liverpool Corporation, of all the existing tramlines. The exchange took place for £30,000, even though the system was valued at £122,000. There were some who wondered if the days of the trams were already numbered.

Expansion and electrification

In 1879, when the Corporation bought the whole of the Liverpool United Tramways and Omnibus Company (the business born of the merger) there were

only thirty cars and 360 horses on a network which stretched from the Pier
Head out to Bootle, West Derby and Wavertree. The process of electrification was
begun in 1898, managing to take in all 75 miles of track and seventeen routes
by 1902. Finally, Brodie's vision of spreading the population out to the suburbs
was becoming a reality. The introduction of affordable 1*d* fares and fixed stops in
1899 made the system even more attractive to the suburban residents, and 101
million passengers were carried in the single year of 1901. The last horse-drawn
car entered the sheds for the final time in 1902, and the Liverpool network was
joined to that in St Helens to create the south Lancashire Tram System.

Although the First World War had greatly disrupted normal life, in the 1920s
the trams were injected with new energy as part of the post-war reconstruction
effort. New facilities were built and the network redeveloped. Throughout that
decade and the next, modernisation of the system continued, even as the rest of
the country invested in a move from trams to motorbuses. For this reason fuel
shortages in the inter-war years were not as much of an inconvenience to commuters as they would have been, although services were reduced to save energy
and manpower. By now the network served as far as Bootle and Kirkby.

The Second World War was not as kind on the trams as the First had been.
The Corporation decided that buses would be up and running and serving the
populace more quickly than a revamped tram system. In addition, a massive fire at
the Green Lane Depot in 1947 destroyed sixty-six trams (10 per cent of the fleet),
many of which were new state-of-the-art vehicles such as the Green Goddesses.
In 1948 the transfer from trams to buses was approved, and a timetable for the closure of the tram routes drawn up. The final journey of the last tram took place on
14 September 1957, followed by a procession of thirteen 'baby grand' trams along
route 6A from Bowring Park to the Pier Head.

The tram landscape

The tram network began as an Inner Circle with two routes out to Walton and
Dingle. At its height it stretched from the Pier Head to Bootle, West Derby,
Woolton and Garston. The main terminal was the one at the Pier Head, where
three loops allowed the vehicles to turn around before starting their return
journey. There was a terminal on Smithdown Road (opposite Cramind Avenue)
with a capacity of 96 cars, operating from 1899 to 1936, which was the second
electrified depot. The first was the Dingle, which opened in 1898 and closed in
1952, with a 101-car capacity. It sat on a site behind the Ancient Chapel, but has
since been demolished. The biggest depot was the tramworks on Edge Lane, just
east of the Wavertree Botanical Gardens. Erected in 1926 many of Liverpool's
most modern trams were built here, and this was the final destination of the last
tram in 1957.

The trams ran on rails out into the suburbs, many along specially constructed
central reservations in the middle of the modern dual carriageways. The roads
themselves have changed little, and so the grassed-over reservations reveal the

The main tram routes across the city converged on the Pier Head, with a terminus which had three loops for the vehicles to turn around on before their journey back into the suburbs. The Pier Head therefore maintained its role as the hub of the town, providing a location for passengers to transfer to the ferries, Overhead Railway or the Mersey Railway. (English Heritage (Aerofilms Collection))

routes taken, and can be seen stretching down East Prescot Road from Knotty Ash to Prescot, and Mather Avenue in the south of the city. Until recently, the distinctive posts holding up the grid of wires which powered the cars still existed as street lights on Horrocks Avenue near Speke. Old tramlines are occasionally exposed by roadworks when the tarmac is lifted, as happened on Tithebarn Street in 2009. Falkner Street, site of an older, horse-drawn tram, shows evidence of the rails having been removed from the cobbled street and filled in. These 'ghost' tracks are visible moving onto Hope Street, where they disappear below the newer road surface.

Liverpool's trams were an essential means of transportation in the nineteenth and early twentieth centuries. They helped open up suburbia before mass ownership of cars, and so shaped the city during one of its greatest phases of expansion. So tied together are the suburbs and the trams that the roads still in use today reflect the curving shape suitable for tram travel, with central reservations revealing old routes. In turn, as new tram schemes are proposed for the city, it may be that the fossilised tram landscape provides suitable sites for this unique mode of transport.

The tramways have left traces across Liverpool. The central reservations they used to pass through the outskirts of town are still present (such as here, on Walton Hall Avenue), and in some places the lamp posts which doubled as support for the electric cables were still in place. In Falkner Street the remains of an older tram system are still visible in the irregular pattern of cobbles running onto Hope Street.

AIR TRAVEL

Air travel was extremely new in the early years of the twentieth century. At first, limitations of the technology meant it was suitable only for wealthy hobbyists, and short flights in England or across the Irish Sea. Later on, mail was taken by plane, and the practical applications of flight began to become clear. By the middle of the 1920s Northern Airlines were operating a daily service carrying mail from Aintree (the racecourse acting as an airfield) to Belfast, with passengers being carried for £3. The short-lived Liverpool Maritime Aerodrome at Garston Docks operated a service to Rock Ferry Pier, but only managed around a fortnight of operation, from September to October 1928. In 1927 the Liverpool Organisation (partly financed by Liverpool Council) had begun to lobby for a municipal aerodrome. At the same time the Air Ministry was putting pressure on local authorities to develop plans which included this burgeoning mode of transport.

Five sites were proposed for the airfield, including two within the area eventually occupied by the first airport, one on the site of the present John Lennon Airport, another in the Woodend Avenue area just to the north, and a final site within Walton Hall Park. It was on 1 August 1928 that Speke Airport's life began, when Liverpool City Council bought 2,200 acres of the Speke Hall estate from the executors of its last owner Miss Adelaide Watt for the purpose of building industrial units and housing. The site of the longed-for aerodrome had been decided. The attraction of the Speke site was that it was an open area close to the edge of Liverpool (Speke was not to become part of Liverpool until 1932), with room for the necessary buildings and landing strip. The flat land was also relatively fog-free, promising reliable conditions for flying. Central government granted a loan of £162,150 to purchase much of this, with the rest being paid by the city in 1933.

Construction began in March 1930 on what is now known as the 'northern airfield' and Speke Airport officially opened on 1 July 1933 (although scheduled flights had taken place since construction began). The first incarnation of the airport was very basic, with a grass airfield and farm buildings used for terminal and hangar space. But rising traffic for Speke meant that more permanent buildings were required, and these appeared in the form of Edward Bloomfield's distinctive control tower and curved terminal building constructed between 1935 and 1940.

As with many Liverpool developments, the life of Speke Airport was interrupted by the Second World War. As the city was a prime target for the Luftwaffe, Speke Airport became RAF Speke, and was held for military use until 1961. It was in this period that the basic grass airfield was replaced with a hard surface, permitting heavier aircraft and creating less drag on takeoff. Under the control of the Ministries of Air and Aviation, further expansion was delayed even after the end of the war. This allowed Manchester Airport to overtake Speke, behind which it had lagged in the mid-century.

The original terminal building for Liverpool Airport is no longer part of the complex, and was redeveloped into a hotel in the early part of the twenty-first century. The apron, on which several aircraft are permanently sat, is still intact and forms part of the Grade II listing which protects the building.

The 1960s saw the dawning of a new age for Speke, as air passenger numbers across the country began to grow. The airport passed into the control of Liverpool Council once again, and soon benefited from a new phase of investment. A £3 million runway extension in 1966 brought the new transatlantic airliners to Liverpool, and allowed the airport to be open around the clock. This new runway had been opened to the south-east of the existing one, due to space restrictions at the old location. A year later a new hangar was built next to the new runway, on the site of the current John Lennon Airport, and passenger numbers increased steadily over the next two decades.

The old terminal was finally abandoned in 1986, with all new developments taking place on the 'southern airfield'. It was left derelict for twenty years, until the late 1990s when it was converted into a hotel. The adoption of a strategy attracting low-cost airlines saw Liverpool enter a period when it became one of Europe's fastest growing airports. This rebirth also saw a rebranding as John Lennon Airport, new links into the local transport system via Liverpool South Parkway railway station, and its runways and taxiways reconstructed for the first time since they were laid in 1966–67.

The landscape of air travel

An airport can be seen as an island within its hinterland: although cars and trains may deliver passengers to its terminals, an airport rarely expands beyond its own footprint into the landscape beyond. But looked at another way, Liverpool's airport can be seen as a barometer of local landscape development. The 1930s, the decade of its birth, were years of expansion for Speke, with its new role as an industrial hub for Merseyside (alongside Aintree and Kirkby). If industrial expansion was something of a departure for Liverpool-as-transport-hub, then the building of an airport was the continuation of its old role – an attempt to keep Liverpool at the forefront of technology, and to connect with the new industrial estates which were to characterise twentieth-century development in this area of the city.

Liverpool was historically well-placed to sit on the route between Ireland and England, and Speke as a consequence was too. Speke's importance as an air base stemmed from its mother city's role as a port, particularly in times of war. Like the grand ships which docked at the Pier Head in the Victorian era, Liverpool's transatlantic links were pursued in the new medium of air travel from the middle of the twentieth century. In the next century the old northern airfield may be turned into a business park, a characteristic development for such an out-of-town area. It would simply be a new phase along a journey that Speke has been making ever since it was identified as central to Liverpool's commercial future in the 1920s.

EPILOGUE

This book has attempted to reveal the role that the landscape has played in the development of Liverpool and Merseyside, and how humans have responded to and, in turn, reshaped the landscape for their own ends. It is clear how the landscape we see today is the sum total of all the changes which have taken place to the landscape over more than 10,000 years.

Although the early history of Merseyside was focussed on West Derby in the east and the Wirral in the west, the coastal geography of the medieval manor of Liverpool meant that its future as a port was almost inevitable. It's important to avoid seeing Liverpool's rise to Victorian prominence as pre-determined, a natural evolution of fishing village to global trading hub. But as this book has shown, a combination of factors allowed the city to specialise in this one function, and it became the source of its great wealth as well as its weakness when trade moved elsewhere.

LANDSCAPE IN THE TWENTY-FIRST CENTURY

As Liverpool enters the twenty-first century, it remains under the influence of what has gone before, and what has been written into its streets and on the minds of its people. Liverpool's resurgence at the end of the twentieth century, which continues today, has drawn heavily on its history – on the mercantilism, determination, humour and artistry – which came from being a river-centric, seafaring city at the crossroads of many journeys. Its economic fortunes now rest on a celebration of its history and culture, which both owe their distinctiveness to Liverpool's place in Britain.

On a city scale, the developments which have begun in the past ten years (and will likely not be finished for decades) can only have taken the shape they do because of the landscape as it was around the turn of the millennium. Chevasse Park, site of the new Liverpool One shopping centre, was once the site of the Customs House, and before that the Old Dock. Only this sequence of development, culminating in a rare open central space, would allow such a masterplan as Liverpool One to be conceived and carried out. Similarly, Liverpool's great number of abandoned docks provides huge areas – and sturdy Victorian buildings – for regeneration. The Albert Dock was the first and most famous example of this, but as of 2013 Peel Holdings, owners of much of the dock estate, wish to completely reinvent the derelict North Docks, albeit treating them as a blank slate on which to superimpose a grand vision of skyscrapers and marinas.

The creation of a precinct on Chevasse Park has raised questions about the landscape of the town centre. On the positive side it bridged the rather large gap between the central shopping area of Lord Street/Church Street and the Albert Dock, the Kings Dock Arena and the new Museum of Liverpool. But on the other hand it moved the focus of the town centre further west, risking the fortunes of the likes of Bold Street, Lime Street and London Road. This awareness of the effects of town planning on the landscape is a mirror image of this book's historical perspective. It seeks to answer the questions: what can past landscape changes teach us about our potential impact when developing the city? How can we do our best to ensure that our current efforts don't become outdated quickly, like many of those 'improvements' of post-war rebuilding?

HERITAGE PROTECTION LAW

For that reason, town planners and developers must consider not just the economic effects their new buildings have on other areas, but also their impact on the existing urban fabric. The 'modern' landscape is actually a combination of every historic change which has gone on. Archaeologists call this a 'palimpsest', a word originally meaning a document on which words are repeatedly written, erased, then rewritten. The end result is a parchment which shows faint traces of everything which it has carried since it was made. Liverpool's landscape, with its eighteenth-century Bluecoat Chambers and its Beetham Tower, its motorways and its original seven streets, is a great example of a palimpsest.

Modern heritage protection laws try to protect this unique blend of features, no longer simply judging whether a single building can be demolished or individual monument torn down, but also whether new developments will have an effect on the landscape nearby. The clearest reflection of this is in the designations applied to whole areas, rather than to specific structures. Whereas the earliest (Victorian) laws protected 'scheduled *monuments*' and later 'listed *buildings*', now Conservation *Areas* and World Heritage *Sites* take in whole cities, towns and landscapes. We also have Historic Landscape Characterisation (HLC) projects, which take large areas of the country and map historic land use. This is not in order to protect or preserve everything with 'old stuff' in it, but rather, as the name suggests, to take stock of the character of the area as a whole. This information can be used by archaeologists, developers and planning committees to judge the effects a new addition to the landscape will have.

Now that we know that any change in the landscape, however small, has some sort of an impact on the surrounding area, we've created tools which help us to measure and predict these effects. The hope is that, as well as protecting valuable historic gems for later generations, overwhelming new additions to the urban fabric fit in with and enhance the quality of the landscape. More importantly, rather than simply act as a veto, designation and landscape considerations allow the inevitable change to happen, but in a way that enhances the quality and distinctiveness of a place.

THE UNIQUE HISTORIC LANDSCAPE OF LIVERPOOL

The history of Liverpool is written in the landscape: in the land-forms, the buildings, the street names, the accents, the music and the faces of the people. It's forever changing, but it's also forever building upon the legacy of 10,000 years of human habitation. Whether you're a born and bred Scouser or an interested visitor, when walking through the streets of the centre, the suburbs, the parks or the docklands, keep an eye peeled for the traces left by those who went before. The 'historic landscape' *is* the landscape, layer upon layer laid down by successive generations of builders and inhabitants. Although there is never a moment when the city should be preserved as-is, the distinctive nature of Liverpool is one to be cherished, perpetuated and protected.

If you've ever taken a longer look at a Liverpool building or streetscape, and thought to yourself 'only in Liverpool', then the chances are that you are absolutely right.

BIBLIOGRAPHY

BOOKS AND JOURNALS

Aughton, P., *Liverpool: A People's History* (Lancaster: Carnegie Publishing Ltd, 2003)

Belchem, J. (ed.), *Liverpool 800: Culture, Character & History* (Liverpool: Liverpool University Press, 2006)

Cowell, R.W. and R.A. Philpott, *Prehistoric, Romano-British and Medieval Settlement in Lowland North West England: Archaeological excavations along the A5300 road corridor in Merseyside* (Liverpool: NMGM, 2000)

Hollinshead, J.E., *Liverpool in the Sixteenth Century: A small Tudor town* (Lancaster: Carnegie Publishing Ltd, 2007)

Patmore, J.A. and A.G. Hodgkiss, *Merseyside in Maps* (London: Longman, 1970)

Picton, J.A., *Memorials of Liverpool, Historical and Topographical, including the history of the dock estate, vols. i: historical and ii: topographical* (Liverpool: G.G. Walmsley, 1875)

Sharples, J., *Liverpool* (Yale: Pevsner Architectural Guides and New Haven and London: Yale University Press, 2004)

The Journal of the Merseyside Archaeological Society

WEBSITES

Historic Liverpool   http://historic-liverpool.co.uk
Liverpool Landscapes http://liverpool-landscapes.net

ACKNOWLEDGEMENTS

Although there's only one name on the front of this book, a project such as this is more than the work of just one person. There are many who have inspired, advised and otherwise helped me with my writing.

Firstly, for their help in digging photographs from their archives and for their kind permission to reproduce them here, my thanks go to Roger Hull and the Liverpool Record Office and the staff at the National Monuments Record in Swindon (now the English Heritage Archive). I'd also like to thank Dave McAleavy, for permission to reproduce the amazing photo of some of the Formby footprints. For permission to use photos from their archives and from existing publications, my thanks to Jeff Speakman, Rob Philpott and Ron Cowell of the National Museums Liverpool Field Archaeology team, and Dave Roberts of the Merseyside Archaeological Society.

A great big thank you must be given to my family: Mum and Dad who greatly assisted on trips around Liverpool, and held umbrellas while I took the photographs for this book (all photographs, unless otherwise stated, are mine), and my wife Sue who created the fantastic line drawings and maps throughout, and proof-read everything from the very early stages.

Thanks to the staff at The History Press – the editorial staff of Michelle Tilling, Emily Locke and Ruth Boyes, and the countless others who brought this book to fruition.

Thanks must also go to all those who I've met in the many years since I started on my historic and archaeological career. They've been crucial in keeping up my enthusiasm, as have all those who've discussed and commented on my websites Historic Liverpool (http://historic-liverpool.co.uk) and Liverpool Landscapes (http://liverpool-landscapes.net) alongside the related Facebook and Twitter pages.

Of course, all mistakes herein are solely my responsibility.

INDEX

Printed by Amazon Italia Logistica S.r.l.
Torrazza Piemonte (TO), Italy

11769765R00094